THE HEALING POWER
OF THE DRUM

THE HEALING POWER
OF THE DRUM

Robert Lawrence Friedman

White Cliffs Media • *Reno, NV*

Disclaimer – The contents of this book do not constitute medical advice. The techniques discussed in this book may impose stressors on the body which involve certain health risks. The reader is advised to consult with his or her physician before attempting any of the techniques discussed in this book and should attempt the techniques only with the advice and approval of his or her physician. In addition, though various techniques using drums and rhythmic devices may have provided benefits for those mentioned in this text, this book does not purport that the methods used will provide the same psychological and/or physiological benefits for others.

Orders from individuals, music accounts and catalogs, libraries, and international accounts:
White Cliffs Media, Inc.
5150 Mae Anne Ave. #213-208   Tel: (775) 674-1671
Reno, NV 89523   Fax: (760) 875-6202
Web: www.wc-media.com   Orders: (800) 359-3210
E-mail: wcm@wc-media.com
    Distributed to the book trade in the USA and Canada by:
Words Distributing Co.   Tel.: (510) 553-9673
7900 Edgewater Drive   Fax: (510) 632-1281
Oakland, CA 94621   Orders: (800) 593-9673
E-mail: words@wordsdistributing.com
    Distributed to music stores internationally by:
Mel Bay Publications, Inc.   Tel.: (800) 863-5229
#4 Industrial Drive   Fax: (636) 257-5062
Pacific, MO 63069   E-mail: email@melbay.com
    Distributed in northern Europe by Airlift Book Company, UK
    Printed on acid-free paper in the United States of America

Friedman, Robert Lawrence, 1957-
    The healing power of the drum / Robert Lawrence Friedman
        p. cm. -- (Performance in world music series ; no. 14)
    Includes bibliographical references and index.
    ISBN 0-941677-87-7 (alk. paper)
        1. Music therapy. 2. Musical meter and rhythm 3. Drum—
Instruction and study I. Title. II. Series
    ML3920 .F836 2000
    786.9'111--dc21
                                                    00-043333

The Corporate Tribal Meeting

While leading my first drumming workshop at a Fortune 500 corporation in New York, I witnessed for the first time the extraordinary power of rhythm to transform and heal. Fifteen employees were playing hand drums in a semicircle when, without warning, a middle-aged vice president suddenly and spontaneously leapt from his seat. With absolute glee he jumped and danced like a gazelle from one end of the boardroom to the other. The usually sterile room was suddenly transformed into a glorious bridge between the contemporary and the ancient, when celebrations always led to dance. The others remained transfixed in their own rhythms, oblivious to the executive, as if this were a daily occurrence in corporate America.

As the program ended, the participants described their own sense of joy and amazement at their ability to release their stress and pent-up frustrations into their taut-skinned drums.

The drum's ability to provide significant healing only become apparent when I received a call a few days later from the dancing executive. He informed me that his intense chronic back problem of many years had completely disappeared during the workshop. Six months later in a follow-up call, I learned that his back pain had not returned. What medications and modern science could not cure, this ancient healing tool had. Perhaps we will never know what specifically caused this executive's back pain to disappear, yet it was clear that dancing to his rhythm and acting on his joy had miraculously altered his body and set in motion a physiological change that allowed him to be pain-free for the first time in a decade.

This executive's experience became just one of many instances when I had the privilege of watching an individual's ailment naturally disappear through the healing power of the drum.

Dedication

I dedicate this book to my mother, Sylvia, a woman of great depth, wisdom and love, a woman who embraces her inner child and sees beauty in everything and everyone. She is the world's diplomat, who like the drum, connects and unites with all who cross her path. She has always encouraged me to follow my inner rhythms, wherever they may have led.

Acknowledgments

I would first like to acknowledge my life partner, Braden Brown, for her extraordinary talent in both revising and copyediting, for the endless hours she devoted to helping me create this book, and for her unyielding support, without which this work surely would not have been written.

I would like to thank Dr. Shi-Hong Loh for his support in bringing the drum into the world of complementary medicine and for his willingness to share his life philosophies with me.

I would like to acknowledge the many researchers who provided their theories and studies of how rhythm enhances health, including Dr. Kenneth Aigen, Barry Bernstein, Dr. John Burt, Dr. Charles Butler, Tom Dalton, Dr. Barry Quinn, Tony Scarpa, Christine Stevens, Dr. Michael Thaut, Dr. Connie Tomaino and Alan Turry. I would like to thank the drummers and drumming facilitators who shared their thoughts, wisdom and stories of the power of the drum, including Jim Anderson, Barry Bernstein, Bob Bloom, Nathan Brenowitz, Randy Crafton, Rob Gottfried, Jim Greiner, Arthur Hull, Heather MacTavish, Babatunde Olatunji, Layne Redmond, Happy Shel and Christine Stevens.

I would like to thank those individuals who shared their stories with me including Melodee Gabler-Tsafas, Connie Gulotti, Ginger Graziano, Thomas Willett and William Roberts.

I would also like to acknowledge the many other researchers, music therapists, and drumming facilitators who are not in this book, but who are nevertheless effecting positive change in others through their work. I would like to credit Rip Peterson for creating his amazing drum circles which provided inspiration, and the gracious pool of drummers who shared their drumming experiences with me.

My thanks go out to those before me who began this journey of drumming and health, including the Rhythm for Life organization, Mickey Hart, Barry Bernstein, Dr. Alicia Ann Claire, Bob Bloom, Randy Crafton and many others who have devoted years of their lives to the pursuit of uncovering the numerous health benefits of rhythm.

I would be remiss if I did not mention Brenda Nicholson, for our timeless connection and eternal soul friendship, Dr. Jennifer Lamonica for her extraordinary wisdom, beauty and love, Lynne Sherbondy, for her unwavering support, friendship and laughter, and Tony Scarpa, MA-CMT, whose positive attitude and enthusiasm helped to shape my vision of the possibilities of drumming and health.

I would like to acknowledge those individuals who inspired me on the path of creating this book, including Jack Abernathy for his relentless support, Dr. Dorothy Firman for helping me gain clarity about my life's rhythms, and Larry Aynesmith for believing in this project, that of merging alternative medicine with the power of the drum.

Lastly I would like to acknowledge my family—my mom, Sylvia Friedman, my brother, Dr. Jeffrey Friedman and my sister, Elyse Glenn for their always present love, my nephews and first two drumming students, Andrew and Jonathan, and my father, Phillip Friedman, who will forever remain in my heart.

Robert Lawrence Friedman

CONTENTS

PART III
Bringing Drumming Into Your Life – 143

Chapter Ten
Practical Techniques and Rhythm Exercises – 145

Chapter Eleven
Drumming Exercises from Music Therapy – 158

Chapter Twelve
Conclusion – 167

References – 171

Rhythm and Percussion Resources – 174

Index – 188

Foreword

Shi-Hong Loh, MD, Director, Complementary Therapy Department, Bon Secours New Jersey Health System

Taoism was introduced to me when I was in eighth grade. It was included as part of the curriculum in education in Taiwan. I was interested and attracted to it because of the philosophy that it implies. Effortlessness, simplicity and naturalism are its key concepts. I tried to "unite with nature," as suggested in Taoism, by wandering in the woods outside the little town where my family lived, lying on top of a big rock looking at the blue sky, daydreaming, watching the branches of the trees waving with the wind and letting the afternoon sun penetrate my body.

Then the drumbeats from a nearby Buddhist Temple would remind me that it was dinner time. I would pick up my bicycle and ride home to my mother's dinner. Taoism was too much for a 14 year old boy to truly comprehend. Yet, the seed was planted.

Throughout years of my practice in oncology, I found myself constantly surrounded by anxiety, depression, frustration and fear of death from both patients and their families. I started to realize the inertia of modern medicine, which subsequently led me to explore other alternatives for my patients.

The major deficiency of modern medicine is that it recognizes only the physical part of a human body, whereas the driving force—mind, soul and spirit—is generally neglected, or excluded from "physical" medicine. This is a very serious problem. Within this erroneous context, not only do we have difficulties in finding better cures for our ailments, but we are also denying ourselves the Whole Being that we are. This is a fundamental mistake of modern medicine.

In my practice of oncology, I noticed many patients developed cancers after they had suffered from very stressful and devastating events in their lives. Many of them developed cancers after they lost their loved ones from ailments, tragedies, or even cancers. This led me to believe that the mind/body connection is the most delicate and important link itself that affects bodily health, either for better or worse.

A few years ago, I attended a convention that emphasized alternative/complementary medicine. One night I passed by a room where a drumming session was in progress. I held my two daughters' hands, one on each side. One was four years old, the other was three. Upon hearing the drumbeats, we couldn't help but start dancing along and laughing. We were so excited that we all tripped and fell together. The drumbeats had touched something deep inside of us. Since then, I have gained a better understanding about the drum and its potential impact on human beings.

The drum is well-known in all races and cultures. Throughout human history, the drum has been used for many musical and non-musical purposes. That the shaman uses the drum to facilitate trance is a well-known example. The drum is a necessity in many religious rituals. The drum is used as a means of communication in some regions. Drumbeats are used to "pump up" an adrenaline surge in foot soldiers before they charge for hand-to-hand combat.

Why does the drum have this power over us?

In fact, it is not the drum, it is the beat. We were used to the heartbeat of our mother even before we were born. It is a well-known observation that the baby feels more relaxed when his head lies on the mother's chest. This phenomenon can be explained based on psychological or emotional factors.

But can the drumbeat initiate some kind of direct physical effect onto our cells by its vibratory effect? After all, our body is made of cells and molecules which, by principles of physics, sustain some vibratory effect from a sound wave transmission. If so, what kind of effect should be expected? What kind of frequency would be optimal to produce a desirable effect? The questions go on.

As much as we like to claim victories in modern medicine, we are still troubled by many ailments for which we don't have solutions, such as AIDS, cancer, Alzheimer's disease, just to name a few. In cancer therapy, we are still using medications that are older than one generation. Tamoxifen, which is the most widely used medicine for breast cancer, was first used in the late 70's, and 5-fluorouracil, which is still considered the most effective chemotherapy agent for colon cancer, was first developed in 1957. It is time to explore other "alternatives" for healing.

A few years ago, I invited drumming facilitator Robert Lawrence Friedman to lead a drum circle for healing in a hospital workshop which was attended by more than seventy people. I was astonished at the effect of the drumming. Everyone was so overwhelmingly driven by the drumbeats that it seemed nothing else mattered. One could easily see that there was only one language used there: the beat, the rhythm that originated from the inner self.

During the session, I noticed the drum generating a unique communication among the participants. I considered this to be a very important step in healing. To be able to communicate with another being requires self-recognition, and self-recognition is essential for healing to take place.

Unlike other forms of mind/body practices, such as meditation, which most people consider difficult to practice, drumming provides an easier approach, and yet, the results can be profound and long-lasting. Especially among children and people with mental or physical disabilities, drumming would be a most suitable and rewarding therapy to enhance the healing process.

Reading Robert Lawrence Friedman's book, I was deeply touched by many stories from the participants of drumming. They are truly fortunate to be helped by drumming facilitators and therapists like Robert Lawrence Friedman, when conventional medicine fails to provide effective treatment for their ailments. I was amazed at the response of a boy with autism and deafness towards drumming. Perhaps one could explain that the response of this boy was made possible by the transmission of the sound wave through the bony structure of the inner ear. Even so, this should lead us to another level of understanding about our perception, about the potential impact of the beat, the rhythm.

In truth, we actually cannot "hear" sound waves, we perceive them. When a sound wave hits our ear drum, the vibratory message is sent to our brain. The brain then determines the significance of this message, "translating" the message into our own learning experiences, for example, "This is the noise of a car," or "This is a beautiful song," etc. One may wonder: Did that boy hear the drum through his heart or his brain?

In our body, we have a lot of organs that are capable of producing their own rhythms—Electrocardiograms (EKG) show the rhythm of the heart, electroencephalograms (EEG) show the rhythm of the brain, and electromyograms (EMG) show the rhythm of the muscle. What should we expect when the rhythm of the drum meets the rhythm of the muscle, brain or heart?

In this book, Robert Lawrence Friedman has elaborated on and added new insights to our understanding of drumming as a tool to enhance healing. In addition to the heart-filled passion and wisdom from the stories in this book, I am certain that readers will find some new insights into the healing potentials of the drum, the beat, and its impact on our own Being.

His programs at St. Mary's Hospital prove that Robert Lawrence Friedman has mastered the power of the drum and its ability to transform. The power and healing qualities of the drum are demonstrated by Mr. Friedman's work with the drum. This book provides many insights about drumming, and readers will certainly learn how to use the art of drumming to improve their health and create greater wholeness. Drumming is an expression of ourselves, the inner self, because we are the origin of the beats. So, the drum, in fact, is more than a drum, it is a vehicle for healing.

Shi-Hong Loh, MD

THE HEALING POWER
OF THE DRUM

PART I

The Limitless Healing Drum

Chapter One

Hand Drums and Healing

When the word "drum" is uttered, most people imagine a person sitting behind a drum set crashing out rhythms while a band plays on. Until recently, the words "drum" and "transformation" would rarely have been used in the same sentence. Yet the humble and relatively unknown hand drum—not the aforementioned drum set of smoky bar fame—is fast becoming an instrument used by people of every age for personal transformation, psychological and physiological healing, and creating community.

The use of the hand drum in relationship to healing is certainly not new. The hand drum has been used for thousands of years in celebrations, rituals and ceremonies. However, the merging of science with the healing qualities of the hand drum is a relatively new development. According to anecdotal reports and current research, the hand drum and its rhythms have been instrumental in improving illnesses when medical science had few answers.

Hand drums are drums from around the globe that are not played with sticks, but which, as common sense would suggest, are played with one's hands. These drums, represented by a plethora of countries and continents, include the African djembe, djundjun, ashiko and talking drum, the Latin American conga, South American surdo and pandeiro, the Middle Eastern doumbek, the Japanese taiko drum and the Irish bodhran and frame drum, along with many others.

Psychological and Physiological Applications

Some of the psychological applications in which hand drums are being used include assisting veterans to release the emotional pain of Post-Traumatic Stress Disorder, releasing the pent-up anger and negative emotions of "at-risk" adolescents, promoting health in corporate employees through releasing their day-to-day stress, and assisting substance abusers in increasing their communication skills and social interaction. Drums have also been used with a spectrum of major mental illnesses, such as manic depression and multiple personality disorder, to increase self-esteem and create feelings of accomplishment.

In the medical field, the hand drum is being used to help Alzheimer's patients improve their short-term memory and increase social interaction, and to help autistic children increase their attention spans. In some cases, it is not necessarily the hand drum that provides positive changes in an individual, but a rhythmic device such as a metronome, or an audiotape which plays specific rhythms. Such tools are being used to aid Parkinson's patients and stroke victims to regain the control of movement or increase their gaits.

Personal anecdotes from both individuals with various illnesses, music therapists and drumming facilitators show the hand drum's ability to have positive results on individuals with conditions such as autism, Down Syndrome, Multiple Sclerosis, paralysis, and even cancer.

As a drum facilitator and psychotherapist, I have personally witnessed the power of the drum to relax the tense, energize the tired, and heal the emotionally wounded. I have also observed the hand drum's extraordinary and consistent ability to create states of euphoria, induce trance, promote play, release anger and promote feelings of community and unity.

There is a burgeoning body of scientific research which points to the drum's ability to promote well-being. Although some of the information I will present to you in this book will be anecdotal, I will also present compelling material from numerous researchers, music therapists, drumming facilitators and other experts in this exciting field.

The Symphony of Rhythm

In speaking with numerous medical doctors, psychologists, music therapists, drumming facilitators, and others, it is clear that the "rhythm field" is wide open. There are many parts to be played, each one no more valuable than another.

The researchers I've spoken to are extremely committed to the pursuit of scientific data. They provide the credibility that allows individuals to consider rhythm as a viable option for health and wellness. Music therapists, like everyone I've spoken to in this area, are genuine helpers. Their specific training and education provides them with a unique vantage point, a wide array of musical options, with the drum being but one of the primary tools of their work. Finally, drumming facilitators, some of whom are trained as counselors, others trained as drummers, all have a similar calling and desire—to use rhythm and the drum to help awaken in others the many extraordinary qualities that drumming can provide, be it joy, release of pain, a feeling of connectedness and unification, a deeper connection to spirit, or the creation of a rhythm community—all possible through the beat of the drum.

In any musical symphony, there are many instruments, each speaking its own voice, yet each vital to create the nuances of tone and timbre necessary to create the musical score as a whole. So, too, then, each of the researchers, music therapists, drumming facilitators and others you will meet in this book are all part of the orchestration of the healing drum and are a portion of the fabric of this rhythmic tapestry.

I have had the privilege of interviewing some of the true pioneers and researchers who have devoted their lives to the study of rhythm and health, including Dr. Michael H. Thaut, Director of the Center for Biomedical Research in Music at Colorado State University, who has used rhythm devices to help Parkinson's and stroke patients gain greater control of their movements, Dr. John Burt, who worked with Post-Traumatic Stress Disorder and Vietnam veterans, Barry Bernstein, whose work with Alzheimer's patients using rhythm-based music therapy pioneered the work with this population that continues today, Christine Stevens, who has studied the use of the drum in relationship to Alzheimer's patients, autistic children and addictions counseling, among other applications, Dr. Connie Tomaino, who works with a variety of neurological disorders using rhythm, Dr. Kenneth Aigen, and Alan Turrey, co-directors at the Nordoff-Robbins Center for Music Therapy, who provided information on their work with children, and Tom Dalton, a music therapist who works with children and bereavement.

My hope is that through examining the breadth of work that is available we can realize that the application of rhythm and its ability to heal the body, mind and soul is boundless. Yet much more research is necessary to confirm what many have experienced and studied already—that rhythm in relationship to the body and mind has many benefits—an idea that our society is just beginning to grasp.

Many of the stories you will read are quite extraordinary and moving. Some are anecdotes of individuals who experienced the drum from a personal vantage point, such as an illness that was improved or grief that was released and transformed into joy. Others will share the touching stories of their clients, patients and workshop participants.

Who Should Read This Book?

This book is written for anyone seeking new channels of creative expression or alternative avenues to address maladies of the physical body or emotions. This book is written for anyone who wants to personally discover how joy and relaxation can sound when they are played.

This book is written for those individuals who believe that the path of complementary medicine is an important one to consider as an adjunct to traditional medicine. This book is written for those educators who would like to examine new ways of dealing with the anger of young people, employers and employees who would like to discover new approaches to managing stress in the workplace, and health care professionals who are open to the mind, body and spirit connection as a way to health for both those for whom you care for and for yourself.

A patient from The Franciscan Home in Jersey City drums
in a workshop with Robert Lawrence Friedman.

My goal in writing this book is to provide the latest research on the healing power of the drum. There may be numerous researchers I did not include. This field is so expansive that there are many worthy topics that this book does not cover. Nor do I provide a lengthy history of organizations such as Rhythm for Life, which was dedicated to the exploration of the drum as a viable vehicle for health, or the many cultures that include the drum as part of their healing rituals. Rather, my goal in writing this book is to provide an overview of the current uses of the drum and rhythm as healing tools.

For anyone who feels that he or she should have been included in this book but was not mentioned, I invite your future participation. Time constraints precluded my pursuing every lead as I would have liked. For those of you who would like to contribute to future books with drumming stories or would like to see additional topics covered in future books, please feel free to email me with your stories and comments.

I invite your inner skeptic to read this book, for sometimes it is only through welcoming the part of us which discerns truth from fiction that we can discover our own truth. If you have ever been touched by the drum, through hearing or playing one, or if you have been touched by someone else's experience with a drum, this book is for you. If you are open to new avenues of healing, meditation, spiritual evolution, team-building, stress relief, anger management, and experiencing more joy in your life, this book is for you.

In this century, when we seem to be moving farther and farther away from ourselves and our deeper needs, the drum, through its simplicity, effortlessness and naturalism, like the Tao, offers us a link back to that which we knew before technology separated us from our soul.

Through providing a channel back to our deeper nature, the drum concurrently provides those who use it with a link to others. The drum seems to have the capacity to unite all individuals who choose to experience it together. Despite race, religion, color, creed, background, or ideology, all are joined together through this ancient instrument's calling. The drum, therefore, becomes a vehicle for transporting all who utilize it across all boundaries, to an experience of wholeness and community.

It is my wish that this book provide you with the desire to seek out a drum or rhythm instrument, learn to use it in a way that allows you to find your deeper Self, to express that which was inexpressible, to tap hidden strengths and abilities that may have been lying latent within, but, once awakened, will serve you in ways you never thought possible.

My hope is that this book will teach you to harness the healing power of rhythm. May the drum help awaken your soul.

Chapter Two

My Journey to the Drum

There's a Baby on the Drummer's Path

My mother told me I drummed in her womb. Naturally, I can't verify this, but I believe her, for wherever I go, whatever I am doing, I am always drumming. Therefore, playing in her womb doesn't seem so farfetched to me. Now if playing drums pre-birth isn't testament to how easy it must be to play a drum, I don't know what is.

My first clear memory of my drumming path was when I was six years old…in my bathroom! I was excited as I stood with my mother and heard my older brother and sister outside of the room scurrying about with my father. It was my birthday and something special was going on. (Birthdays were a big deal in my family.) The bathroom door finally opened and on the floor was a seemingly endless series of large red cardboard arrows leading to some destination in our home.

"Follow the red arrows, Bobby," my father urged. With great excitement and anticipation I walked alongside the arrows. "The arrows will lead you to your present, but when the arrows stop, you'll need to find your gift." The arrows finally ended in front of a large cushioned chair. With my small fingers, I lifted a seat cushion to find the gift that would forever change my life—a drum practice pad constructed by my father and two wooden drumsticks. From that moment forward, my life was in the hands of rhythm.

Though I didn't realize it then, this drum pad would serve many psychological purposes for me as I grew up. My parents, though very loving to their children, spent a fair amount of time yelling at each other. The pitter-patter of my drumming on my drum pad helped to release my stress and pain. I believe this rhythmic buffer zone prevented me from taking on the pain of my parents' conflicts. Conversely, when I had moments of glee, I would gloriously beat my joy into the pad, and hearing the sounds reflected back to me somehow magnified my good feelings.

Drumming Away My Mother's Migraines

Having a mother who was a migraine sufferer could have been a problem for a drummer, but my mom's surprising reaction to my drumming planted the first seeds of my belief that the drum provides healing. My mother, Sylvia, shares her thoughts on migraine headaches and the drum.

> I recall my son drumming while sitting in his high-chair as a very young child. My family and I listened in disbelief when he would drum to music in perfect cadence. But a mother who suffers with severe migraine headaches having a son who is a talented drummer—this sounds like a recipe for disaster.
>
> Nonetheless, I was soothed by the reverberation of the drum as he practiced. Whenever I had a migraine headache, if I listened to his drumming, my headache would often gradually disappear. This fact was greeted with disbelief by my doctors. Nevertheless, it was true. I was mesmerized by the rhythms of the drum and somehow they caused my migraines to dissipate. It is because of the drum that I discarded my migraine medication. The power of the drum is sheer magic.

I had a fairly traumatic adolescence, serving as the chosen victim of a group of boys, masquerading as friends, who knew I didn't want to fight. I was picked on frequently, and the drum pad became my vehicle of self-preservation. Beating out my anger while thinking of those kids, this birthday gift created by my father provided me with a vehicle to channel my fury safely without causing myself or others pain.

Finally, when I was 14 years old, I made the empowering choice to leave this group of boys. I spent an entire summer in my home, playing my drum pad. It became a friend whose accessibility and power comforted me. Through hitting the pad, I felt my power resonating back to me. This small rubber practice pad secured and enhanced my self-esteem, for not only was I releasing my pain, but I was also perfecting a skill.

My next evolutionary step took me from the drum pad to the playing of a drum set, the sound of which was much louder than the rubber pad my father had created.

My Fifteen Minutes of Fame...Ouch!

As one of the lead drummers in my high school band, I was setting up my drums for our final concert and putting a drum stand together. One of the clasps plunged into my index finger, causing a deep cut which I bandaged feverishly with a yard of gauze minutes before the concert began. With 500 students in the audience, I excitedly anticipated my final five-minute drum solo. The moment arrived, and as I began hitting the drums faster and faster, the gauze began to unravel in ever-widening circles as if it were a planned special effect. The roar of the crowd escalated into a crescendo in response to my visually exuberant solo. I hardly felt the gauze as it slapped my face over and over again with each beat. (I never figured out if they were clapping for my ability to swirl the gauze or for my drumming.) *The drum has the capacity to excite!*

In my late teens, I began moving towards spirituality and including hand drums in my drumming repertoire. I found that through hand drums the quality of unity could be created fairly easily among strangers. I discovered this by accident when I traveled to various spiritual centers, attending the workshops of spiritual leaders such as Shakti Gawain and Ram Dass.

In one instance, following a Shakti Gawain workshop, I sat alone on the grass at Omega Institute, a spiritual retreat center in Rhinebeck, New York, playing one of my hand drums, a doumbek from the Middle East. I closed my eyes and created a spontaneous rhythm. Soon afterwards just a few feet from me, without invitation, another drummer using a djembe drum began playing a rhythm alongside my own beat. Then moments later, I heard another drum, finding its own beat, complementing ours. Then another and another and another. When I finally opened my eyes, there were a dozen drummers drumming with me—complete strangers, yet linked through this magical and magnetic experience in which, though not a word was uttered, the profound depth of our connection was felt. *The drum creates community.*

On another spiritual occasion, the Harmonic Convergence, I took my doumbek to a mountain in Sedona, Arizona. As scores of drummers pounded their drums in unison atop this peak, people began dancing and, as if moving into deep trance, some fell over backwards, taken over by the power of the drum, the power of spirit. What was it about the drum that caused these individuals to seemingly move into trance in such a deep manner? *The drum has the power to alter consciousness.*

You Did What With Bobby McFerrin? Sing?? Why???

I've had my share of some magical, yet wacky moments drumming. I recall a musical workshop I attended at the Omega Institute in New York. As I waited for the program to begin, I began a particular spontaneous drum rhythm that I felt. As I played my drum, I thought I heard this melodic voice just behind me echoing my rhythm. I turned around and was startled to see Bobby McFerrin, vocalist extraordinaire, singing my beat and finding the spaces between the sounds to create a nuance of rhythm and voice. Of course, as Bobby joined in, it gave others the incentive to drum with this incredible singing master.

After the program, I found the courage to ask him to join me under a nearby tree and play music together. Moments later, Bobby McFerrin and I were warbling together, my drum lying silent and forgotten on the ground. My one opportunity to drum alone with Bobby McFerrin, and I decide to sing with him instead. I must have forgotten I'm a drummer, and not a singer. Admittedly, even he seemed surprised.

Omar Hakim, and Me, or Whose Concert Is it, Really?

The Percussive Arts Society (PAS) is an organization of individuals who support many areas of drumming. In 1994, I attended a PAS conference in Atlanta, Georgia, in which drummers and percussionists from all over the world attended to see the latest rhythmic equipment for purchase and mingle with rhythm greats. As I scouted around an area where the various companies sold their wares, I found two beautiful ashiko drums from a company called West Cliff Percussion, which has since been acquired by Remo, Inc.

I purchased the drums and heard that there was going to be a concert that evening with Sheila E and her family of musicians. This being my first PAS conference, I assumed that everyone would be bringing the drums and rhythm instruments that they had purchased that day and would at some point join Sheila E and her band in some kind of audience participation spectacle. The spectacle was not to be with Shiela E.

When I arrived at the concert with my girlfriend, our drums in tow, we discovered, embarrassingly, that we were the only concertgoers with drums. Nevertheless, as unobtrusively as we could, we took our seats and waited for the concert to begin, unrealistically hoping no one would notice our drums. This was not to be the case.

As I glanced to my right, to my amazement, I realized that Omar Hakim, who had been Sting's drummer, was sitting just two seats away. He asked me if he could play my new ashiko drum. I didn't want to deny this master my drum, and as drums often do, it seduced him into starting a rhythm—a quiet but very rhythmical beat. Of course, I couldn't let him play alone. I requested my girlfriend's ashiko, which she surrendered. Emerging from the murmur of the crowd, our rhythms danced together, and, to the security guards' dismay and the crowd's delight, we began getting louder and louder (the crowd mostly being interested in Omar, of course).

At first, the security guards looked disparagingly at me, but upon seeing Omar, they relaxed, for someone famous was entertaining the crowd prior to the beginning of the concert. The rhythms became more complex as our drumming became its own concert. I felt as if Omar and I had entered a sacred space together, where time stood still.

I would have thought this moment couldn't get more extraordinary, but suddenly the drummer from "They Might Be Giants," who was sitting in between Omar and me, began scatting to our rhythms. All three of us were locked into this very spontaneous mini-concert. Reality then interrupted our session as the lights dimmed and the concert began. Though Sheila E's concert was great, it was my own concert with Omar that made PAS a memory that will last forever. *The drum provides moments of magic.*

Despite my obvious love for drumming, my mom, a practical woman, convinced me that drumming should not be my primary vocation, so I chose another passion, psychology. I completed my Master's Degree, then continued on to Advanced Certification in Psychosynthesis, a holistic approach to psychotherapy. It wasn't long after beginning my counseling work with individuals and groups that I realized that merging my two loves, drumming and psychology, was my true path.

The Experiment Begins

Due to my recognition that the drum provided me stress relief and numerous other benefits, in 1986 I purchased 100 hand drums and called the New Age Health Spa in Neversink, New York, in order to try an experiment to see if these benefits could be experienced by others. I asked the program director if she would be open to my proposition. I suggested a one-hour workshop in which the guests learned to play hand drums, followed by a relaxing guided imagery. To my delight, she agreed.

A month later at the spa, my day had arrived. Entering the carpeted workshop space, the spa guests, an assortment of professional people, were greeted with exotic drums, one resting on each chair. The participants, though at first reticent, quickly became comfortable and excited with their new instruments. At their own pace, the spa guests began touching, feeling and hitting their colorful rhythm instruments, without my prompting.

After some simple drumming exercises and instruction, within an hour, the entire group was creating wonderful rhythms. It was harmonious and joyful, and they seemed to love it.

I followed their intense drumming session with a relaxing guided imagery exercise in which I had them close their eyes and imagine themselves lying down on the warm sand of a beach. I found that by combining drumming with a guided visualization exercise, many guests were able to achieve a much deeper state of relaxation than ever before.

My theory is that the drum provides an active release of tension, while the guided imagery provides a passive form of relaxation and the combination of using both techniques provides an optimal environment for inducing a deep state of inner calm. Since that experience, I have continued to travel to the spa monthly to offer my program, "Drumming Away Stress." This combination of drumming and visualization consistently evokes the same unusual feedback from participants: the feeling of having two seemingly mutually exclusive states of consciousness simultaneously...being both highly energized and deeply relaxed. In addition, individuals who had resistance to relaxation in the past reported that they were able to relax enough through the drumming to be able to, for the first time in their lives, vividly experience a guided imagery.

Two years at the spa and hundreds of new drummers later convinced me that I had something that worked, and I decided to form a company called "Drumming Away Stress, Inc.," currently "Stress Solutions, Inc." In the past five years, I have introduced the drum as a vehicle for team-building, stress and anger management to corporations, hospitals, high schools, camps and conferences.

Though I deeply enjoy doing my drumming programs for executives and laymen in varied settings, some of my most rewarding work is now through my affiliation with St. Mary's Hospital's Department of Complementary Therapy located in New Jersey, which is run by the Medical Director, Shi-Hong Loh, MD. Through this progressive medical department, I am bringing the healing power of the drum to Alzheimer's patients in nursing homes, at-risk adolescents in detention centers and homeless shelters, former substance abusers in halfway houses, community leaders in nearby housing projects and to both children and adults in the surrounding neighborhoods.

The Drum Unites Parents and Children

One Saturday morning during a drumming program for children in the community at St. Mary's Hospital, I was encircled by ten children, each with his or her own history, some orphans, others with their mothers and fathers sitting in the back of the room. As I gave them drums and we began playing, their drumming styles immediately reflected their personalities. One boy, Bob, expressed his interest in being a rock musician, hitting the drum exuberantly to assure me of his commitment to this goal. Three girls, orphans, all looked down when a reference was made to someone's mother, each hitting the drum quietly, their personalities shut down through the pain of not having a mother to call their own.

Called upon to express their emotions, some children played their drums fiercely, letting out the pain of years of isolation, while others played with lightness and abandon, sparkling with their joy still intact.

As I drummed with the children, I began watching some of their parents in the back of the room, smiling, tapping their feet, moving their bodies to the rhythms they heard. I knew I had to invite the parents to participate as well. Why exclude them from experiencing this joy and having the opportunity to connect with their children in this way? Handing out drums to the mothers and fathers, I realized that there was very little difference between the parents and the children. Both felt embraced by the beat. Soon all were enveloped in the web of the drum's power. The rhythms merged as everyone became part of the greater whole. In that moment, there were no orphans, no parents, only people set free to express their excitement. For a brief moment, old pains were forgotten, hope was affirmed, and life held endless possibilities. *The drum eliminates boundaries of separation.*

Drumming and Oneness

In another workshop, I met with fifteen African-American women from a housing project. Each one of these women performs a role of service in their community; they are the pioneers seeking to make the lives of those around them better.

As I shared my knowledge of drumming with these women, they all remained open and respectful, yet seemed slightly amused at having a thin, bespectacled Jewish guy teaching them how to play African drums. It was a poignant and ironic moment. However, any resistance faded as the powerful drums became the only presence felt. At one point as we were playing, I felt like we were in a revival meeting as each woman let out the pain of trying so hard to help others while at the same time trying to find peace within herself. The rhythms that issued forth from their fingertips communicated their strength of conviction. Their power was reflected in this instrument of tradition, embedded within their roots, shared by a welcome stranger whose skin color, momentarily, was the same.

The Drum – So Powerful, Yet So Simple

I can honestly say that I never bring drums and people together without several people coming up to me afterwards, expressing wonder, excitement, and even euphoria. The credit belongs to the drum, the magical, sacred drum, which has the extraordinary power to touch something deep and powerful within all. It awakens an aspect of ourselves that lies dormant until it hears an ancient calling through the rhythms of this healing vehicle. These sounds awaken our spirits and speak to our most primal and truest selves.

The drum touches that part of us that knows nothing of cell phones, faxes and deadlines. This part of us to which the drum speaks knows only inner peace, self-expression, and that which is our very basic life force. Drumming creates an island in time, where all else is shut out except the rhythms that issue forth from your fingertips at your pace, expressing your feelings at that present moment. Is it any wonder our souls hunger for it? The only wonder is that a need so vital could be supplied by a vehicle so simple—the drum.

Chapter Three

The Ancient Calling

Technology is the science of arranging life so that one need not experience it. –Anonymous

The more caught up in technology we are, the more we need to maintain a connection to nature. When I present my "Drumming Away Stress" workshop at the New Age Health Spa, I meet many individuals who tell me that they come to this spa, located in the mountains of upstate New York, because city life doesn't fulfill them, yet nature absolutely does. There is an emptiness within many that needs a resolution. It is this emptiness that the drum and its rhythms, symbolically and literally, fill.

Arthur Hull, recognized as one of the pioneers of the drum circle movement, describes what occurs when a culture embraces rhythm. It becomes, in his words, a "rhythmaculture."

A rhythmaculture is a culture that uses rhythm, dance and song in ritual form that permeates the lifestyle of the people in that culture. You know you are in a rhythmaculture when the music and rhythm permeate the major life events among people. The rhythms have a purpose and take the form of ritual. Most of the rhythms that we study from around the world are still very much alive and used. Rhythm is not a dead language. Especially in Africa, every rhythm that you study has a purpose.

As a musician, I study the rhythms to be able to play them. I study rhythmaculture in order to import the universals of rhythm into the growing rhythmaculture we are birthing in the United States today. Through rhythmaculture, you start to understand that there is purpose behind every rhythm and with every rhythm there are dances, and with every dance, there are songs. As our Western culture is in the process of developing its own rhythmaculture, it is also in the process of discovering the drum and rhythm as a tool for healing.

A continent that clearly has a rhythmaculture is Africa. The many African cultures include many societies in which the drum permeates practically every aspect of life.

Master Drummer Babatunde Olatunji came to America in 1957 and is credited with introducing African drumming to America. His first record, *Drums of Passion*, became a classic musical composition highlighting the importance of rhythm in society.

In the following passage, Baba, as he is lovingly referred to throughout the world, graciously shares his words of wisdom on the power of the drum in African society.

Words from a Master Drummer – An African Perspective

The drum was a primary form of communication in Africa. It was used for socialization, entertainment, dancing, communication and healing.

The foundation of African music is the drum. The whole village uses the drum. It covers all of the vicissitudes of life.

In terms of communication, if I am 25-30 miles apart from someone on a farm, I may pick up the drum and say, "I'm leaving" through my drum. The sound travels so far. You may say, "Where are you going?" and I respond, "I am going home" all by playing the drum. The other farmer would say, "Well, then, I'm leaving, too."

The drum can help you get to your Self, your centered Self. Every cell in your body and mind is in constant rhythm and when sound touches it, something happens to you. The emotion that the vibrations of the drum create in you can be negative or positive. Through drumming you can create rhythmic patterns that make people jump up; you create rhythmic patterns that make people hold hands, and the drum allows them to feel soothed. That's an indication of the evocative power of drumming.

The sound of the drum resonates with an inner chord that vibrates through your whole body, so that when you go through the act of drumming you are energizing every cell in your body.

Drums have been in existence in one form or another throughout time, either through body percussion or the clapping of hands or the stomping of feet. That is what started it.

Because of the drum's capacity to duplicate sounds, anything we hear or see we can replicate through the drum. We can imitate sounds of birds or the flow of rivers, even waterfalls through the drum. Those sounds have always been around us.

Drums have been around through the ages. If you read *Twelfth Night* by Shakespeare, Shakespeare described many different types of drums. He said, "If Music be the food of love, give me the excess of it." The excess of good music will not hurt you. How did Shakespeare get to that understanding? I discovered he spent a lot of time in Africa. He described drums that were found everywhere in the world.

First of all playing the drum gladdens my heart. I feel more than satisfied. I feel accomplished. Many times a person will say, "Baba, I was standing right in front of you" while I was playing a drum. But I didn't see him. I see you, but I don't see you. My attention is right on what I'm playing, and sometimes I have to stop if I find myself getting out of my physical body. Hold on, let me come back to earth. I forget all of my worries, all of my pains. When I feel hurt emotionally, I get on the drum right away. My drum is my best friend; nothing else can soothe my spirit like the drum.

What I call the language of the drum refers to the many tonal qualities on one drum. Because of the tonal quality of the African languages, whatever you say verbally, you can repeat on the drum. In African society, we used the drum before Ma Bell was discovered. The drum was our telephone. It was our form of communication. We used the drum in this way because of our belief that if you can say it, you can play it.

You don't have to be an Andre Agassi to play tennis, and you don't have to be a great musician to play the drums. People play the drums because they love to play the drums. They play for socialization, bringing people together—that's what the drum does.

One thing about the drum that I love is that if you put all kinds of instruments in a big room, most people will look at the drum, then play it. Though at first they won't want to play the drum, something in them makes them do it. I tried it with children. They look at the drum, then stop, then hit it hard. The drum is a very powerful instrument. The force of exertion that is generated by the drum is extremely powerful.

The body of the African drum is carved from the trunk of the tree. There has to be spirit in that wood, it's not dead wood. You can tell the difference between dead wood when you throw it in the fireplace and it burns. Another kind is the wood that you put in a fireplace which stays there all night till in the morning. There must be a spirit in the carved body of the drum. Ninety-five percent of the time there is a spirit in the skin. Otherwise you won't get a particular sound. We tried it many times. If a particular goat skin is not tanned very well, it won't give you a sound. It is the spirit of the person playing it that becomes an irresistible force against any moveable object.

Your spirit, the spirit of the skin of the drum and the spirit of the wood all join together in playing the drum—that is the spirit of the drum.

I am doing a research project with 40 psychologists and psychiatrists at the University of Naples in Italy. We are using the drum with patients in a hospital. These people are losing their minds, and they don't make any sense when they speak. But for two days, we put them in groups with the drum and within an hour, they are talking, answering questions, laughing. I am very excited about this research and its results.

The Hungry Soul

As we move into the 21st century, it becomes apparent that our society has largely relied on technology and materialism to sustain us. Yet, through all of our technological advances, there persists a deep and ever present need to find happiness and fulfillment, meaning and purpose in ways that technology simply does not offer. Despite its impressive marvels, technology does not have the capacity to provide us with meaning and purpose. As we have embraced technology, we have forgotten that one of the great needs we have as individuals is to be heard, to find and create simplicity and to make connections of the heart, mind and soul with others. The drum fulfills all of these needs.

The drum provides us with an ancient form of communication, one that does not rely on the articulation of words, but one that uses a much more basic language, our emotions expressed through sound. When you hit the drum hard, it can be an expression of anger. When you hit the drum softly, it can be an expression of fear or contemplation. It is this basic simplicity of expression that makes the drum a perfect means for children and others who may censor or repress their emotions because they fear judgment or feel unsure of how to express their feelings in words.

The drum seems to awaken the recognition of a spirit within. Yet often the soul's calling goes unnoticed. We feed our body when it gets hungry, yet we do not see the signs and cues that our soul gives us when it is hungry. The emptiness, the hopelessness within our society, serve as signs and symptoms that our collective soul needs to be fed.

Our soul is not fed by reading negative newspaper stories and viewing news accounts of pain and suffering on television. Our soul is not fed by technology, no matter how extraordinary the advances may be. Our soul is not fed by closing our minds and hearts to love and its many rhythms and manifestations.

The soul is fed through turning our attention within, through connecting with others in ways that reflect depth and purpose, and through play and laughter. The soul is nurtured through connections of the heart. The drum provides all of these needs. The hand drum serves as a touchstone to our deepest nature. It is both a symbol of our spirit and a vehicle to transport us into it.

The soul is fed through opening ourselves to our innate connection to nature. By taking a drum under the trees and imagining that the beats you play are Nature's pulse—the indescribable power that pushes the grasses up through the earth and transforms sunshine into wild flowers—you feed your soul.

The soul is fed through connecting heart-to-heart with your community. Though playing the drum in groups, a sense of togetherness is nurtured. I have seen groups of from 20 to 400 people become as one almost instantaneously in harmony and love through the simple act of hand drumming.

What is it about the drum that creates this feeling of connection so completely and quickly? When people communicate verbally, they are limited to one person speaking and others listening, and there is great room for miscommunication and misinterpretation. When a group of people are drumming together, everyone is speaking through his or her drum and listening to the drums at the same time. What occurs is a symphony of intertwining rhythms in which everyone is speaking, everyone is heard, and each person's sound is an essential part of the whole. Thus the drum becomes a tool of empowerment for all who partake of its gifts.

Through playing a drum with others, several things happen simultaneously. When we hit the drum and make our sound, the drum helps us find a personal creative expression. Through unleashing ourselves into this skinned instrument, the drum induces inner joy while simultaneously providing us with a connection to ourselves and a deeper connection to others. Through playing a drum, we connect to a physical object that is not battery-operated and has no assembly required. In this moment in history when we are enveloped with advances that tend to separate us from ourselves, we can welcome the drum as an object that emerged from nature and magically helps us to remember our own rhythms, which are a reflection of the deeper pulse of nature itself.

The rhythm we make when we play the drum with another is like an aural hand shake, yet the connection goes much deeper. It can even be likened to a soul embrace. This embrace can encompass a room filled with people of all ages, races and creeds. When we play drums with others, vibrations enter through our ears, caress our bodies, massage our organs, dance within the cells and jiggle the soul back into remembering itself.

Rhythm, Both Within and Without

If you could see your DNA, you'd see what your inside rhythm looks like. You are rhythm. You are made of flesh, blood, bones –and rhythm. Rhythm is what keeps you alive. –Mickey Hart

Within our bodies, we have the rhythm of our breath, juxtaposed by the rhythm of our heart. There is the rhythm of our blood flow and our brainwaves. There is the rhythm of the menstrual cycle, and the constant firing of our neurons. Within each of us is a symphony of rhythms. The very first sound we all hear is the constant, enveloping rhythm of our mother's heart.

If we take a step outside of ourselves, there are universal rhythms occurring all around us. Every 365 days the earth revolves around the sun, while every 28 days, the moon revolves around the earth. Every 24 hours our planet rotates on its axis. Since the dawn of time, these cycles have intertwined and are the background against which our universe exists. Whether we are aware of them or not, rhythms exist both within us and without. Arthur Hull discusses his thoughts on rhythm.

> Rhythm lives within everyone, and it's not something special. People don't have to have professional musical talents and techniques to express their rhythmical spirit. Everyone has a rhythmical sensibility within and how they express it is differs from person to person. Rhythm permeates everyone's life. It is in everything we do, we see, we feel, and it is within the circadian rhythms of our bodies, as well. Rhythm is a fact of life.

In The Beginning, There Must Be Rhythm

Experts are beginning to believe that rhythm is critical for human development. "We are born with a need for rhythmic input," says Kay Roskam, Ph.D., director of music therapy at Chapman University in Orange, CA. "It affects how our brain waves function and may play an important role in normal physical, emotional and intellectual development." According to Dr. Roskam, infants who receive steady, strong rhythmic messages through rocking, coupled with loving sounds from a caregiver, have quicker visual and auditory development, and, she states, music therapists note that lullabies in every culture use a repetitive, slow, steady pattern that seems to have a universally soothing effect.

Jim Anderson, is a licensed Marriage and Family Therapist in Irvine California, the owner of Percussive Innovations, which manufactures music therapy products, and Rhythm-Power! which is a company that runs corporate and youth drum therapy seminars. He has studied the effects of rhythm on our day-to-day lives, including rhythms that are physical, psychological and social in nature. He says that rhythm begins to affect us as early as birth.

Following are some of his thoughts on rhythm and its primal effects on human beings.

> When a baby is born, its mother attempts to synchronize with its needs, feeding it when it is hungry, putting it to bed when it is tired, and soothing it when she sees it is fretful. Ideally, the mother and infant fall into a rhythm in which most, if not all, of the baby's needs are met, and the baby develops a sense of trust and security regarding the world around it. If, for whatever reason, the mother or primary caregiver is unable to synchronize with the physical and psychological needs of the child, the baby may develop negative coping mechanisms, such as withdrawal or aggression. These tendencies can become part of the child's personality and color all its future social interactions.

The rhythms of life continue, according to Jim Anderson, and affect us throughout our lifetimes. A questionnaire which he has devised to help individuals evaluate how rhythm impacts their lives appears in Chapter Eleven.

Shifting the Sands of Time

Dr. Stephen Rechtshaffen in his popular book, *Time Shifting,* explains that we become entrained, or synchronized, with the rhythms around us. If, for example, we work in a busy, stress-filled office, our inner rhythm may become one of pressure and stress. If we are walking down Madison Avenue in New York at rush hour, we may walk quickly matching the pace of everyone else even if we are on vacation and have no reason to walk quickly.

To avoid becoming entrained in rhythms that don't serve us, Dr. Rechtshaffen has devised a technique he calls "Time-Shifting," which allows us to become aware of the rhythms which are affecting us and make a conscious choice as to which we will choose to synchronize with.

He tells us how to create "pause buttons" at work that remind us to stop our frantic pace, breathe, and come into a rhythm that is comfortable. He makes suggestions for switching from the rhythm of the office to the rhythm of family life or relaxation by the use of simple rituals. The rhythms at which we move through our lives can make us feel relaxed and fulfilled or stressed and unhappy.

Rhythm is a Given

Randy Crafton is a performer, composer and teacher of rhythm and music. With an impressive array of recordings to his credit, he is on the faculty of The World Rhythm Center at The Drummers' Collective in New York and the New York Open Center. He travels throughout the country presenting workshops and master classes on rhythm and drumming for Remo, Inc., Crafton Percussion Works, All One Tribe Drums and Rhythm for Life. He shares his thoughts on rhythm.

> Very few things are a given, but rhythm is a given. We should embrace it, utilize it and enjoy it. Since the beginning of recorded time, rhythm has been used for entertainment, to create a sense of community, to define ritual space and to heal both physical and psychological maladies. Rhythmic singing and drumming are the basis of many ancient and even some modern healing techniques. These traditional techniques of healing through rhythm are rooted in personal intuition, experience, and the collective knowledge of the community. I believe there is without question a place where these techniques and laboratory-based methods of modern science can meet and agree.
>
> Everything we perceive is based on rhythm. Some of the slower rhythms are the changing of the seasons, the rising and setting of the moon and the orbit of the earth. Our bodies are a symphony of rhythms, some are so fast that they produce sound frequencies and some are so slow we can barely detect them. Among the inner rhythms most easily translated into musical terms is the heartbeat, which normally is in the range of 55-85 beats per minute. The rhythms of healthy human bodies will have consistent rhythm ratios, such as the breath cycling in a ratio of 4 to 6 heartbeats for every in and out breath. Slowing the breath often acts to slow down the heartbeat, and vice versa.
>
> In music and rhythm, there are certain rhythms which are very pleasing to our ears, such as the polyrhythms 2:1, 3:4, and 3:2. They affect us physically and psychologically in very positive ways

because they echo rhythms which exist within all of us.

To be healthy our internal rhythms must be synchronized with the environment. The widely accepted Cosmic Receiver Theory states that the human organism is not only in rhythm with itself but is attuned to the large scale rhythmic structure of its environment. A living organism is, at one level, a very delicately balanced rhythmic machine and yet it is highly adaptable to many environments and physical challenges. Our bodies could be compared to factories that are rhythmically synchronized for optimal production. One cell cannot secrete what another is not prepared to use. When these relationships are not synchronized, we become sick. Often when we are not feeling well, we say, "I am feeling a little out of synch."

Entrainment is the tendency of objects moving in a similar pattern and tempo to align with one another. Scientists have recognized this tendency through simple experiments. The most classic example is that of two swinging pendulums which over time gradually align and begin to swing in unison. Nature adheres to the law of entrainment on many levels. When birds fly together in migration patterns, they will flap in rhythm together and glide at the same times. Women who cohabitate can confirm that their menstrual cycles often synchronize over a period of time. Once we begin to observe its influence on our environment, our minds, and our bodies, we can easily see that there are many levels at which our lives are profoundly influenced by rhythmic entrainment.

Through reflection on the rhythms of our universe, the rhythms of our society, and the basic rhythms of our bodily processes, it becomes very clear that there is nothing outside of rhythm.

Chapter Four

The Personal Experience of Drumming

Rhythm permeates everyone's life. It is in everything we do, we see, we feel, and it is within the circadian rhythms of our bodies, as well. Rhythm is a fact of life. –Arthur Hull

Finding Your Drum

In order for you to fully experience the depth of the benefits that drumming provides, you need to play the drum for yourself. Finding your drum can be a joyful endeavor. There are many possible goals in seeking out your first hand drum.

The first decision is whether to look for a drum that reflects your personality as it is now or to find a drum that reflects the personality you are trying to cultivate. Is it to be used for building your confidence? Deepening trance? Movement? Healing? Each intention may set your path towards a different drum. Once you are clear about your intention, then trust the direction you choose. Allow your intuitive mind to direct you.

Do you want a large djembe or conga drum whose booming sound can express your self-confidence and power, or a frame drum whose voice is more subtle and nuanced? Do you want a drum that produces sonorous, majestic sounds or a "talking drum" that can express your feelings through a variety of tones? Do you want a colorful playful drum or a simple wooden drum? Do you want an ashiko drum from Africa or a ceramic doumbek drum from the Middle East? In each case, you will want a drum that feels right, has the right touch and the right feel for you. Do you want a drum that is made from cherry wood or a drum that is manufactured and has an attractive design? Don't rush the process! Hit the drum, make a sound. Hit it in various ways. If you will be carrying the drum a lot, you may want a lighter drum, perhaps a single-headed buffalo drum or bodhran.

Sometimes individuals will use the drum to help them attain a higher state of consciousness. Some people call this evolved state, the "higher self." This aspect of self has qualities such as kindness, compassion and love. When you choose the path of the drum as a way to seek your higher self, it is important that the drum you choose be one that reflects that Self that you are seeking, in color, size, sound and vibration. In this way, it is important to trust your instincts and not get caught in another's ideas about what you need.

Drumming Alone

When you play your hand drum alone, there are numerous benefits. Your drum can help you develop creative expression. It can also be used as a tool to quiet your inner voices, for instance, self-criticism, fear or doubt. Drums can also help to unlock the emotional blocks that you may have, that may be repressed or suppressed within. There are exercises at the end of this book designed to assist in that process, though I always recommend when dealing with the emotional process to work directly with a trained music therapist or counselor.

Drumming in a Group

Playing drums with a group of people or even one other person has enormous benefits. The drum can be the ultimate non-verbal communication tool. When you play in a drum circle or with other individuals, you need to learn to both listen and play, always being aware of what the group is creating and your place in it. This form of playing can be quite inspirational. In many drum circles that I have attended, a group synergy is created that unifies and transcends the individuals involved. I have seen many circles where when the rhythm has ended, the silence creates an extremely positive feeling in the room from which nobody wants to leave. It is as if something sacred is touched through drumming, creating a re-membrance within each person that within each of us is an inner silence that we can embrace.

Playing the drum with others has additional benefits. Playing the drum can help you to build confidence and self-esteem. It can be used to release negative emotions, such as anger, into a safe venue, though it is always important to not hurt yourself hitting the drum when working with painful emotions.

Drumming with others provides a simple yet profound interaction. Communicating without words is the simplest way to communicate. When drumming in a group, we communicate non-ver-bally—with a look, a gesture, body language and the sounds of our beats. Sometimes these expressions are more honest and complete than anything we can say in words. Hitting a drum with others allows for an easy expression of emotions, of anger, joy or community team spirit or whatever an individual may be feeling.

Drumming provides a way of communicating that is beyond prejudice, beyond judgment. It is through the drum that children who do not have an easy use of language and articulation can be heard, their anger felt and shared with others.

Whether we play with others or alone, the drum provides the perfect communication tool, unencumbered by the restrictions of verbal language, and creating an environment where your emotions can flow freely.

Your Joyful Inner Child

Joy is not in things, it is in us. –Benjamin Franklin

Your "joyful inner child" is that part of you that loves to play, any-time and anywhere, and has the qualities of innocence and trust. It is spontaneous and always eager to have fun. Eventually we learned to squelch this part of ourselves as we became adults and took our requisite "serious-training."

When we were in kindergarten, we did not have the same rules that we now have as adults. We didn't think about who was watch-ing us and what they thought or how we would be judged. The joyful inner child is an aspect we can learn to reclaim as we let go of our self-judgments and give ourselves permission to move beyond the constraints of adulthood. It is that part of us that we include as we recognize that, in order to be healthy, we must learn to cultivate our ability to play and live joyfully. The drum can be a delightful catapult towards this goal.

When I encourage my workshop participants to give themselves the freedom to relax and let go into the drum, to make-believe that they are kindergartners, magic seems to happen. When adults allow themselves to remember the best experiences of being a child, a more natural self seems to emerge who is trusting, happy and relaxed.

Current research points to the importance of the quality of play to maintain our health. As Hara Estroff Marano describes in her article, "The Power of Play" in *Psychology Today*, play keeps us mentally flexible, promotes creativity and reduces anxiety, and provides many documented health benefits. Marano cites a study of a group of gifted individuals begun in the 1920's which shows that those who are enjoying the greatest longevity are those who have played the most throughout their lives.

The drum provides the perfect outlet for the joyful inner child to play because it requires no training to create exuberant and expressive sounds. Through allowing yourself to simply hit a drum, you then begin a cascading effect in which this instrument becomes the first step in trusting yourself, taking risks, and allowing spontaneous self-expression.

This story by drumming facilitator, Jim Greiner, describes an experience in which a burly farmer has a close encounter with the drum and discovers his joyful inner child.

Heartland Community Drumming – Jim Greiner

In the mid-1990's I was contracted to lead a community drumming program for a major farm belt city's annual civic festival. I was told that they wanted something that would bring people together in a feeling of community celebration to add to their regular line-up of bands, food booths and local merchants. I was also told to not expect too many people to actually participate as this was, after all, "heartland America," and not exactly prone to trying new things." I replied that I learned a long time ago not to expect too little from people when it comes to celebrating community; that, when given an opportunity, people will rise to a level of participation far greater than even they expect. I hoped I was right!

Over 200 people arrived to play! The organizers were astounded. I was amazed. The people who came to drum were ecstatic! I saw people laughing, pointing to one another and saying variations of, "I didn't know you drummed, too!" Co-workers, acquaintances and even members of the same church learned for the first time of each other's love for the drum. They also realized that there had been an unspoken assumption that they had to hide their drumming from other people because they were concerned that they would be thought of as "different." So they drummed by themselves or in small groups, hidden away from disapproving eyes (or ears). That alone was a profound realization for us all.

As I led the group in the first rhythm, assigning appropriate parts to the different families of drums and percussion instruments, I could see more than just a bunch of people drumming together for fun (which is reason enough!). I saw people coming together as a community in the truest sense, that is, a group of people contributing their individual natures and skills to shared goals.

Other people came, drawn by the powerful groove and obvious atmosphere of celebration, until there were several hundred onlookers surrounding the drummers. I started them clapping and singing along with the rhythm until almost 500 people were involved. I caught the eye of one of the organizers who gave me a look that said as clearly as if he had spoken into my ear, "Did I say not to expect too much? I can't believe what I'm seeing!"

Someone later sent me a series of photos of the event with a note that read, "Check out the farmer on the edge of the group on the right side." I looked at the photos, smiling, being reminded by them of the fun we all had that day, and at re-learning (for the umpteenth time!) the lesson of letting go of preconceived expectations. I then looked for the person who was described by the note-writer. I found him on the outer rim of onlookers. He was in his late 50's, a beefy, strongly built man with skin burnt by endless hours spent working in the sun, wearing a baseball cap

Jim Greiner

with a "John Deere" patch. In the first of the photos he stood with his arms folded over his chest, leaning slightly back on the heels of his feet and with an expression on his face that said clearly, "What the heck are these people doing!?" In a later shot he had his hands on his hips as he stood more straight up and down with a curious look on his face. In a later photo he was leaning forward at the waist clapping his hands and had an enormous grin on his face.

I've always wanted to meet that man and ask him what he thought about the drumming and what we all shared that day. I admire him for allowing the spirit of the event to move him, even though it was clearly something new and completely foreign to him. I remember him, and all the members of that heartland drumming community who allowed themselves to be moved by a spirit of community celebration whenever I find myself holding back from trying something just because it's new or different. From then on the term "heartland" always had a new meaning for me.

In some ways, we are all like the burly farmer when we are faced with something outside of our "comfort zone." It is socialization that teaches us to mistrust the new and different. Socialization also teaches us that it is the child who needs to learn from the adults, yet "reverse socialization" is a phrase I have coined that states that we as adults need to learn from our children. Somehow in learning how to be adults, we forget the wisdom of the child. There is great wisdom is trusting ourselves and allowing our spontaneity to express itself in the world.

In truth, the only elements that get in the way of allowing ourselves to embrace this joyful and playful inner child are our own inner boundaries, fears and beliefs. Perhaps we believe if we were to have more fun and let this inner child out, we would be laughed at by those adults who really took their "serious training" seriously. Or perhaps we have gotten so used to not enjoying life that we think that this is normal, particularly when we see everyone else not enjoying life along with us. As adults, many have lost touch with a deep and ever-present need to experience lightness, glee, trust and simple fun. In our "serious training," we have forgotten these primary requirements for well-being. When we are eighty years old, we will not remember our day-to-day working hours, but rather we will remember those moments when joy smiled upon us.

It is the quality of abandon that adults need to cultivate and nurture. In my workshops, one of the goals I have for my participants is to remember the feeling of being in kindergarten. I once offered my drumming program to a group of thirty school teachers. Although they were very resistant to letting go, I gave them drums and asked them to risk being playful. Their resistance was short-lived, for within a short time of doing various drumming exercises, they danced and drummed with abandon. The drum had allowed each one to open to the joyful inner child that existed within. As a drumming facilitator, it is my responsibility to be that which I wish to teach, therefore, by showing the teachers that I was willing to be my own inner child, uninhibited and playful, they were able to risk being theirs.

I've heard that as young children we laughed 300 times a day, yet as adults we laugh only 15 times a day. We certainly need to laugh more. I have realized as a therapist and drumming facilitator that if you want more fun in your life, you need to believe you deserve it. Create it inwardly—through both believing that you deserve to have fun and getting beyond the inner dialogues that say you don't.

When you play the drum, your joyful inner child plays the drum with you—revel in the partnership!

Drumming and the Family

Sometimes you struggle so hard to feed your family one way, you forget to feed them the other way, with spiritual nourishment. Everybody needs that. –James Brown, the "Godfather of Soul"

I recall one of my first experiences in which I created a drumming event for a family. I was invited by a woman to create a rhythmic surprise for her husband who was celebrating his thirtieth birthday. At one point in the evening, I invited all of the members of the wife's family to drum in one circle and the husband's family to drum in another circle. The goal was to create rhythms in which both circles would meld rhythmically. As the rhythms merged, the families, who had had their differences in the past, began laughing, for they didn't recall the last time they all got along so well. The next exercise involved all of them drumming together in one circle. The results were the same—the drum helped to create harmony through its rhythms.

I next had all the men who were thirty years or older create a rite of passage for the husband. In this ritual, the men who were thirty years and over drummed together in a circle and then when the clock stuck midnight, they opened up their circle in order to allow the new member in. This symbolized the welcoming of a new member into their ranks. The husband said that he had no idea that hitting the "big-3-0" could be so much fun.

Every holiday when all of my family members come together, we hand out various drums and play together. This has been occurring for the past 20 years and I really believe that this has helped us remain harmonious.

As a psychotherapist, it has become very obvious to me that many conflicts are due to anger and pain which may represent unspoken thoughts and emotions. Some of these are based on mis-communications, neglect, anger, inconsiderations, and a myriad of other causes. Therefore, any tool that can foster positive communication between people should be explored.

The drum is an excellent tool for working through family issues for a number of reasons. Due to the drum's working on a nonverbal level, it transcends the blockages that hinder communication. Also, the drum can allow negative emotions such as anger to be released. Ideally, a music therapist would assist in this process.

Thus, through drumming out conflict, or simply drumming to have fun, a family opens up the possibility of a new kind of communication which can provide an environment of greater intimacy. Since drumming is fun, it can provide a family with a lighter atmosphere in which conflicts can be more easily resolved and harmony increased.

The Psychology of Drumming

When one looks back over human existence however, it is very evident that all culture has developed through an initial resistance against adaptation to the reality in which man finds himself. –Beatrice Hinkle, Psychiatrist

There are numerous psychological benefits in drumming. First is a sense of personal power. The sound of a drum is power made manifest. Second, the drum places one squarely in the here and now. When a person is worrying, he or she is generally caught in the web of the future or the past. Through hitting a drum, an individual is transported out of the mind and into the body's solidity. Hitting the drum is an absolute definitive action. When hitting the drum, there is no time to think about tomorrow's fears, yesterday's regrets or what's for dinner. The drum places an individual in the present and sacred moment. In this way, the drum is very grounding.

When people play the drum they should try to not hold back in any way; thus the drum becomes an opportunity for those who repress their emotions to release them, for individuals, both men and women, who censor themselves to have full and total (non-verbal) expression. When working with deep emotional issues it is always recommended to do so with a therapist or music therapist who can support you through the process. I recommend using drums that use mallets or sticks when working with releasing emotions since it is harder to hurt your hands with them. Paddle drums, buffalo drums, drum sets, timbales and electronic drums are some of the drums that use mallets or sticks.

In our society, full and total expression on any level is an extraordinary gift, for many of us censor our thoughts and hold back our feelings. One of the gifts that the drum provides is the opportunity to communicate freely.

That the drum can provide a release of unexpressed emotions is related in a story by a gentleman who attended one of my drumming programs.

The Emotional Surprise – Thomas Willett

I came to Robert's drumming class because I had just purchased a drum and wanted to begin to learn how to use it. I had in mind to learn the basics so that I could go to a community drumming circle. We began his class with relaxation exercises to the sound of the buffalo drum. I came directly from a long day of work and with the lights down and the sound of the drum and his encouragement, I was able to do the breathing and relaxation exercises. I found that the sound of the drum, the cadence, the lingering aftertones helped me to relax and focus on deep breathing and letting go of body tension.

He started us all on the simplest of rhythms. To my surprise, the other participants were able to almost immediately begin to do them. He kept the lights down low, and we began to slowly drum in unison to a slightly more complex beat. To our general beat, he improved and led us along.

As the class began to come together, and we all became more used to doing the more complex rhythms, I found that I could relax and just drum, without having to worry about missing too many beats and without fear I could not get back to the rhythm. The lights were low; we had been drumming for about 45 minutes, and the class had a feeling of "flow" or group unity, and there was a strong male lead against which I could play and rely. As I began to go deeper into just drumming without thinking, I experienced a surprising wave of emotional sadness.

Even at the time I experienced it, I was quite surprised. I had thought of drumming as a kind of wild release of energy or tension. I never expected to find drumming to help me release the sadness that I already knew I was carrying around. If anything, I thought that drumming would be an escape from thinking about that sadness I was feeling.

In the last five years, I have had a series of emotional losses and have just begun the process of trying to heal. I have also suffered substantial financial reverses which I'm slowly overcoming. And finally, last weekend my mother with whom I'm quite close had another heart attack and was hospitalized. I had just returned from visiting her and although she was recovering well, I was looking for the drumming as a way to forget about all of these losses and problems.

It therefore came as quite a surprise that I felt the sadness, although not despair. It was feeling sad but without feeling overcome by it; it was feeling that things had been lost and cannot be replaced but not necessarily that the future would be bleak. Indeed, the emotional release of drumming felt like a pathway toward good feelings in the possibility of connecting with other people and having moments, like drumming, when you feel good. In a sense while I felt the sadness, I continued to feel calm and continued to be able to be one with the rhythm and support the rhythm of the group. I had a feeling that riding the wave of the rhythm, riding the waves of the drumming, was like riding the waves toward a better future if only I can stay on the rhythm and use it as a way to release the sadness and feel connected to the pleasure from drumming, and having people to have fun with. I could not have been more surprised by this experience.

Drumming for some reason helped me to release some of the sadness. Like many men after their divorces are final, I felt a surge of interest in many areas. Among them was drumming. As I have tried to describe, the experience of drumming in a setting with a good counselor and with an environment intended for the release of tension helped me to explore my deeper feelings, in particular, sadness.

It does seem to me that a person is able to experience negative feelings like sadness when they are relaxed but also when they feel secure. The security allows them the opportunity to let the negative feelings rise to a conscious level of feeling. In a secure place with the opportunity to discharge those feelings the conscious mind allows the feelings to be felt because it is safe, and there's an opportunity to discharge. Perhaps that is why I felt the sadness when we were drumming. I felt secure, accepted, gaining in competence and mastery, led by a rational, masculine figure, supported by women in the room, kind of proud of myself for what I was doing in the drumming and supplied with a way to let some of those feelings escape.

Every day psychologists validate through research the importance of letting go of the negative emotions we store in our bodies. The drum provides an outlet for this release like no other. The drum allows this release to be completely nonverbal. One of the blocks that exist in many adults is learning to enunciate their feelings, and because feelings are so elusive, it can be very difficult, particularly for men, to let go of old pains, old emotions. The drum can provide a tool for letting these emotions go.

After the words and beliefs that block our heart are released, we are left only with love and the drum helps us to release those blocks. When we let go of our words, we are left with emotions. When we release our emotions, we are left only with sounds. When we release our sounds, we are left only with the drum.

Psychologists have long studied rhythm's effects on our psyches. Roberto Assiogoli, Ph.D., who in 1908 founded Psychosynthesis, a holistic discipline in psychology, devotes a chapter in his book *Psychosynthesis* to music as a healing agent. He notes that ancient peoples used the drum and rattle to increase the effectiveness of herbs and also used the instruments alone to promote healing (Assiogoli, 238)

He cites references in the Bible and the writings of Homer, Plato and Aristotle which indicate the use of music for medicinal purposes (237-238). Interestingly enough, in the nineteenth century, according to Assiogoli, the use of music and rhythm was more appreciated by the military than by healing practitioners. Every regiment had its own band and drummers which kept up the morale of the troops by constantly playing spirited marches.

Dr. Assiogoli calls rhythm "the primordial and fundamental element of music" and refers to the poet d'Annunzio's pronouncement of rhythm as "the heart of music" (239). Assiogoli goes on to say that "rhythm is the element which has the most intense and immediate influence on man, and it affects directly both the body and the emotions" (239).

He notes that in addition to the various rhythms within our bodies and the subtle vibrations of our cells, there are the additional rhythms of our psychological selves, such as the rhythms of elation and depression, sorrow and joy, fervor and lassitude, strength and weakness and introversion and extraversion. He feels that all of these conditions are extremely sensitive to the rhythm of music (ibid).

In the 1930's, Dr. Carl E. Seashore wrote a textbook, *The Psychology of Music,* which is still in print today attesting to the timelessness of its concepts. In a chapter entitled "Rhythm," he discusses the nature and psychology of rhythm.

According to Dr. Seashore, rhythm has the capacity to both stimulate and relax. While rhythm often brings on a mild form of ecstasy, the elation is frequently accompanied by a feeling of relaxation or a feeling of being lulled. This is illustrated by the fact that when we hear rhythmic music, we often feel like dancing. However, once we are fully engaged in the rhythm of the dance, we often become oblivious to our surroundings and fall into a sort of auto-intoxication (Seashore, 142).

A rousing march incites the soldier to snap to attention, stand straighter and take firmer steps. Yet, once the march is well underway, the cadence of the drums evokes a state of passivity and obliviousness to his actions. The soldier can march further and better, listening to the strains of the march with less resulting fatigue (ibid).

When we move according to our innate rhythms, our movements will be confident and efficient. We instinctively know where and how to place our hands and feet without conscious effort. Therefore, a sense of rhythm has life-preserving potential. Anything which preserves lives will tend to become instinctive, as rhythm has for mankind (143).

The fact that rhythm is so deeply ingrained in us may explain why Alzheimer's patients respond to rhythm when many of their other capacities have failed, why small children need not be taught rhythm but respond to it automatically, why Parkinson's patients can often move without "freezing" when a rhythm is played, and why autistic children can briefly come into "our" world and interact with people and things when rhythm points the way.

As Dr. Seashore states, rhythm has benefited us biologically from the beginning of time and is therefore as much a part of our makeup as our respiratory or circulatory systems (Seashore, 143). Rhythm resonates in our emotions as well as our bodies. Thus when we listen to the thundering waves of the ocean or enjoy the rhythmic swaying of trees in the wind, we are emotionally drawn into these scenes and feel ourselves part of them (143-144).

Finally, Seashore observes that the end result of our instinctual craving for rhythm is play. He defines play as "an exertion of body and mind, made to please ourselves, and with no determined end." He believes that rhythm "makes us play, young and old." Because of rhythm's capacity for endless variations, it is never monotonous. As soon as we master one level of rhythmic expression, we are propelled onto the next level, each one becoming richer and more fulfilling (145).

Intuitive Drumming

> *Intuition is a spiritual faculty and does not explain, but simply points the way. –Florence Scovel Shinn*

According to the American Heritage Dictionary, intuition is "the act or faculty of knowing without the use of rational processes." "Intuitive drumming" is trusting that because rhythm is occurring within us at every single moment, we are all inherently rhythm-makers. All that is required is believing that we can externalize the rhythms that are in within us.

One of the most powerful and simplest drumming exercises is to play a heartbeat rhythm on a drum. This primordial beat, echoing the sound we all heard in our mother's womb, will lull and soothe. The beauty of drumming is that, even in its simplest form, it can provide enormous benefits.

When you are in touch with your intuitive drummer, you realize that rhythm exists throughout your being and that your natural inner rhythms will guide you to burst out in joyful, rhythmic spontaneity. If you can allow this intuitive drummer to be a part of your playing, you will not be thinking, "Does this sound okay? Am I doing this right?" Accepting your intuitive drumming, just as it is, becomes a metaphor for accepting other parts of yourself just as they are.

I recall an instance when, at the beginning of a drumming program, an 80 year old woman told me that she always wanted to be a drummer but never trusted that she had the ability to play the drums. Though she was clearly reticent about expressing herself through a drum even now, by vocalizing both her inner rhythms of breath and heartbeat and some external rhythms that she had heard in her rich and varied life, she realized that rhythm was not something foreign to her. She began to play the drum with such verve and excitement that when she was finished the class gave her an ovation. By allowing herself to play the drums, this woman gave herself permission to do something that she had wanted to do but resisted for decades because of societal fears of being ridiculed. She said she felt as if she were 16 years old again…and she looked it!

Entrainment

When a group of people play a rhythm for an extended period of time, their brain waves become entrained to the rhythm, and they have a shared brain wave state. The longer the drumming goes on, the more powerful the entrainment becomes. It's really the oldest holy communion. –Layne Redmond

A few years ago, I took a djembe drum to the center of midtown Manhattan with a friend and his conga in order to perform an impromptu experiment. During the height of rush hour for a two-hour period we played very fast rhythms, matching the tempo of the passersby as they sped past us. The barometer for our success was the number of people who stopped to watch us. What we found was quite interesting. When we played fast rhythms, no one stopped, not even a glance. It seems as if they had no interest in hearing something that reflected back to them the fast rhythms of their stress.

In the same two-hour period the next day, instead of playing fast rhythms, we countered the speed of the walkers with very, very slow, steady rhythms. Almost immediately, people began to stop, smiling as they watched us for a few minutes. The drums' rhythms enabled the passersby to entrain, even for a brief moment, into a more relaxing state of mind.

An interesting note—though we weren't seeking any compensation, a few people placed fruit in front of our drums, perhaps as their way of letting us know that our slow drumming brought them back to a more natural state of mind. What this story introduces is what I believe is one of the primary healing benefits attained through drumming, entrainment.

The Discovery of Entrainment

A Dutch scientist, Christian Huygens, discovered the concept of entrainment in 1665. Huygens found that if two pendulum clocks were placed side by side, by the next day their pendulums would be swinging together in perfect unison.

Christine Stevens, a music therapist and drumming facilitator, states that entrainment is the tendency of people and objects to synchronize to a dominant rhythm. Dr. Michael Thaut, neuroscientist and Director of the Center for Biomedical Research in Music located in Colorado State University explains entrainment in more clinical terms as "the frequency of a moving system being determined by the frequency of another moving system." Entrainment provides us with an explanation of the greatest clarity as to how drumming may provide us with assistance for many of our maladies.

The concept of entrainment also allows the drum to shift individuals out of their current states of mind, if they choose. For example, if a person is feeling lax and tired, they can either play a slow and steady beat that will reflect that feeling back to them or create a fast rhythm that will energize them. Similarly, if a person is feeling stressed and wants to relax, he or she can play slow and steady beats as the body entrains to the slower speed.

Landmark studies were done several decades ago by the scientist Dr. Andrew Neher. Under laboratory conditions, Dr. Neher attempted to test and explain unusual behavior in drum ceremonies. He focused on the effects of rhythmic drumming on the central nervous system, finding that the rhythms of drumming could entrain his subjects' brainwaves into the alpha or theta states. Alpha brainwaves are associated with states of relaxation and general well-being. Theta waves are usually associated with drowsy, near unconscious states.

Layne Redmond, author of *When the Drummers Were Women*, is a well-known teacher and performer whose main instrument is the frame drum. She is also an acknowledged expert on the ancient history of women as drummers and leaders of rituals. Layne shares her expertise on how drumming can unify or synchronize the right and left hemispheres of the brain.

One of the most powerful aspects of drumming and the reason that people have done it since the beginning of being human is that it changes people's consciousness. Through rhythmic repetition of ritual sounds, the body, brain and the nervous system are energized and transformed. When a group of people play a rhythm for an extended period of time, their brain waves become entrained to the rhythm and they have a shared brain wave state. The longer the drumming goes on, the more powerful the entrainment becomes. It's really the oldest holy communion. All of the oldest known religious rites used drumming as part of the shared religious experience.

It is interesting to look at these ancient drumming practices from the perspective of the latest scientific research into the functioning of the brain. Using electroencephalographs, scientists can measure the number of energy waves per second pulsing through the brain. A system of classifying states of consciousness according to the frequencies of these waves was created.

Normal outwardly focused attention generates beta waves which vibrate from 14 to 40 cycles per second. When awareness shifts to an internal focus, our brain slows down into the more rhythmical waves of alpha, vibrating at 7-14 waves per second. Alpha is defined by relaxation and centering. Dropping down to 4-7 cycles per second the brain enters the theta state in which there is an interfacing of conscious and unconscious processes, producing hypnagogic dream-like imagery at the threshold of sleep. Theta is the source of sudden mystical insights and creative solutions to complex situations and is marked by physical and emotional healing. People with a preponderance of theta brainwaves are also able to learn and process much more information than normal. Without some form of intensive training, it is hard to stay awake in theta—one slips quickly down into delta. This is the slowest brainwave frequency, 1-4 cycles per second, the state of unconsciousness or deep sleep.

The brain is divided into two hemispheres that are basically split in their control of the thinking process. The right brain functions as the creative, visual, aural and emotional center. The left brain is the rational, logical, analytical and verbal administrator. Generally, either the right or left brain dominates in cycles lasting from 30 minutes to 3 hours. While one hemisphere is dominant, the memories, skills, and information of the other hemisphere are far less available, residing in a subconscious or unconscious realm. Not only do the right and left brain operate in different modes, they also usually operate in different brain wave rhythms. The right brain may be generating alpha waves while the left brain is in a beta state. Or both can be generating the same type of brain waves, but remain out of sync with each other. But in states of intense creativity, deep meditation or under the influence of rhythmic sound, both hemispheres may become entrained to the same rhythm. This state of unified whole brain functioning is called hemispheric synchronization or the awakened mind.

As the two hemispheres begin to resonate to a single rhythm, a sense of clarity and heightened awareness arises. The individual is able to draw on both the left and the right hemispheres simultaneously. The mind becomes sharper, more lucid, synthesizing much more rapidly than normal, and emotions are easier to understand and transform. The conscious and unconscious levels of the mind interface and integrate more easily. Insight quickens and creative intuition flourishes, giving one the ability to visualize and bring into manifestation ideas more easily. An expanded, more complete and integrated state of consciousness comes into existence. Scientists believe that hemispheric synchronization may be the neurological basis of transcendent states of consciousness.

Research has shown that rhythmic music is one of the most

effective ways to induce brainwave synchronization. Musical comprehension is a joint function of left and right brains and rhythmic sound can drive the brain waves into alpha or theta states. Many ancient religious practices seem to have originated in attempts to induce the transcendental experiences of hemispheric synchronization. Traditional drumming rituals appear to be efficient techniques for entraining the right and left brains, leading to emotionally and physically healing experiences.

The Unifying Quality of the Drum

Seemed to me that drumming was the best way to get close to God. –Lionel Hampton

There is a universality in rhythm that transcends races, cultures and countries. This is highlighted by the following story by Nathan Brenowitz, a drummer and psychotherapist, who discovered that the drum can even bridge hostile countries.

Drumming Up Peace – Nathan Brenowitz

One thing that always haunts me as an American is my total inability around languages. Throughout many years of traveling, I have continuously been awed by people who can speak multiple languages. Naturally, I have always rationalized that Europeans have a real need to change their vocal communication as they move from Italy to France, whereas not much happens when you cross the border from New York to New Jersey. Nevertheless, no matter how much I may rationalize, I still feel inadequate.

This trip was going to be different. My most recent journey took me to the Middle East. My main reason for going was to spend time with one of my sons, Luke, who is currently attending a University in Jerusalem. This city is absolutely one of the most beautiful and diverse places in the world. Almost everyone spoke at least two languages, and most were in the three-to-five range. Then there was me with my Brooklynese English that even the British couldn't understand. I was determined to communicate on an entirely new level, so I brought along an additional language with me. I kept it in my backpack and always had it ready. What was it? Nothing more than a simple, primitive drum! My mission was "peace through music."

Nathan Brenowitz and his son, Matt, drumming together.

Luke and I sipped cappuccino in the cafes, ate the best humus and falafel, played basketball, tennis, chess and wandered through the old city where, as always, I was brought to tears at the Western Wall.

Early one morning, out of nowhere, we decided to go to Jordan. Luke had never been to an Arab country, and he had some definite beliefs that he carried with him. We jumped on a bus and headed for Amman, the capital city. When we arrived we were greeted by a bustling place filled with exciting markets, wonderful aromas and people hurrying everywhere.

We found an inexpensive place to stay and continued our wandering. As we made our way down a small winding street, I suddenly stopped as I heard the rhythmic sounds of my second language coming from nearby. My "voice" was beginning to feel a little bit heavy on my back. I followed the sounds to a rooftop across the street. I went into the building with Luke at my side and climbed three flights of stairs to the roof.

What awaited us there were three young men playing doumbeks, the type of drum played throughout the Arab world. When they first saw us they were momentarily startled, but smiles soon came to their faces as I quickly took out my drum. Without a word I began fitting in a rhythm to their playing. The nods of approval I was receiving let me know I was being understood.

As time passed, we soon established that the spoken word would get us nowhere, as neither of us spoke the other's verbal language. They were most interested to watch and hear my style of playing. Although I also played a doumbek, I held the drum differently, and my style was more Cuban-influenced than Middle Eastern.

Since Luke also drums, we passed the various instruments around enjoying the slightly different feel and sound each instrument provided. The session lasted about two hours during which time we laughed a lot, made great eye contact and developed an authentic mutual respect for each other's playing. Through drumming, we reached a level of relating that for the moment transcended the political.

Luke came to Jordan with certain preconceptions. He is very pro-Israel, and although a peace treaty was signed with Jordan three years ago, his feelings about the Arab people were mostly due to his limited contact. What he discovered were extremely hospitable, intelligent people who worked, played and loved their families just as we do. Stereotypes will most often go by the wayside upon personal contact. This is not to say we would be able to compromise on the burning issues we're all so passionate about. At this time, however, my second language was able to transcend the issues and take us to place of pure communication.

William Roberts, the dojo director of the New York Center of Sukyo Mahikari (a spiritual organization dedicated to the Art of Offering Divine Light), shares his experiences playing the drums.

Drumming: One Way to Tune in With God
– William Roberts

I have been attracted to drums and drumming as long as I can remember. From a very early age, anytime I saw drums of any kind I would get excited. Even when going for a ride in the family car with my parents, the highlight for me was riding by the music store and seeing the drums in the window. Anytime I saw live music my eyes would be riveted on the drummer. There really is no logical explanation for this. (Unless, of course, you believe in past lives.)

As a young boy, I began playing on empty coffee cans with the plastic covers using long pencils as drum sticks. When I was eleven years old, the high school music director came to our grade school to get children interested in playing some kind of instrument. Of course, there was no question! It had to be drums!

I have had many wonderful drum teachers in my lifetime, and I have learned so much about myself and the world through the drums and drumming. For me it has always been a spiritual experience. In essence, drumming allows you to become one with the other musicians and the audience.

Of course, lowly egos can often get in the way with perform-ers—people trying to outdo each other, etc. However, when sincere people truly try to connect with each other in order to create something beautiful for the world and for God, something incredible happens.

One teacher told me that the drum could be considered the very first instrument in that the heartbeat is our first experience in life. We as drummers are charged with keeping the rhythm, which of course, is always here and flowing along uninterrupted. When we truly connect with that universal rhythm, it feels so good. It makes people happy. It makes people dance and it may allow them to be transported to some new level where they can feel hope and find more joy and positiveness in their lives.

According to science, everything in this world is comprised of vibrations or undulations. Therefore, I truly believe that drums and drumming are natural expressions of God and the cosmos. Drumming allows us to reach deep down into the core of our beings and get in touch with a very primal aspect of what it means to be human. This then allows us to connect with—to tune in with—God, the will of the Universe, cosmic conscious-ness, whatever you prefer to call it.

In this sense, as many cultures can attest, drumming also has tremendous healing capabilities. I am no expert by any means, but in my own experience drumming allows me to relieve stress in a very profound and joyous way. In addition, that feeling of oneness of the universe, not to mention the great joy one experiences doing something one truly loves, must inspire the body to create and release endorphins and other healing agents quite naturally. Also, in addition to the wonderful spiritual and mental/emotional effects, it can also be a great physical workout.

I thank God for drums, for all music and for the opportunity to share these thoughts.

The Alchemy of Drumming

The drumming was a very important key to my healing. Drumming at first was a way to heal my grief, but it became a way to remember my joy. –Ginger Graziano

"Alchemical drumming" is the process of transmuting what is unhealthy in the body and releasing it through the drum. Psychology and medicine alike acknowledge that bottling up emotions is detrimental to our mental and physical health. In a thirty year study, psychologist Pirkko L. Graves determined that individuals who suppressed their emotions were sixteen times more likely to develop cancer than those who expressed their emotions freely and took active measures to relieve their frustrations or anger.

Through hitting the drum, unhealthy and toxic emotions can be released. The drum, then, becomes a tool of alchemy, altering that which is negative into something positive through an action as simple as a drum slap.

Arthur Hull shares his thoughts on the drum's ability to release.

Drumming with a purpose is the difference between a light bulb and a laser beam. When people come together to drum, be it in a ritual form, such as a solstice gathering for the changing of the seasons or trance drumming to travel where the mind becomes quiet, or Shamanic drumming where physical healing takes place, then you use the drum as a laser beam rather than a light bulb. When people get together to drum, a vibration occurs and the vibration, like water, seeks its own place to vibrate, soothe and release the tensions and energy in the heart, the soul or the mind. The drum channels expression of all kinds. It is a universal element. Some of those expressions are joy, frustration and anger. A drum can be used to express emotion, whatever variation that emotion takes, from extreme bliss beyond thought to the depths of personal pain and sadness, it doesn't matter. It all comes from the same source, the drum, and it is all a release.

Rhythm creates a vibration. It is like water. Water seeks its own level, and it has a mindlessness. It obeys certain laws of nature such as gravity. It goes to the lowest spot it can find. Rhythm, by the nature of its being, because it is a vibration, has a fluidity. The vibration of the drum travels to the place that needs it the most. This place may be emotional release, physical release, stress release or anxiety release. It is a vibration that is placed in the kinesthetic body. Rhythm travels to and vibrates the place that needs it the most—the mind, the body, the spirit or the soul.

The drum can be a metaphor for our own inexpressible truths. When we invite the drum to express those words or feelings that are unexpressed within us, then it can become a tool for healing.

As this mother discovered after her son died of cancer, the drum can provide an opportunity not only for releasing the unbearable pain of the loss of a child, but also a means to embrace joy.

Healing My Grief Through Drumming – Ginger Graziano

My 19-year old son was ill with cancer for two years and eventually died. One night before he died, a friend and I were at a full moon circle when suddenly two men came out of the woods and started playing on djembe drums. Although moments before I was feeling somber as I reflected on my son's illness, I felt this electrical jolt in my body in response to the drums. I said, "Whoa, what is this?" I suddenly got excited and felt this surge of energy just listening to them. At that moment, I knew that the drum would eventually help me, though at that time all of my energy was taken up with my son's illness.

In the months after my son's death, at first I was very numb. When I realized he had died, I was afraid I wouldn't survive the pain, which was more intense than anything I had ever experienced before. It took me about three months before I was able to face my grief.

I felt I couldn't be in this amount of pain and not feel like dying. I couldn't even fight against it. It was like falling off an edge of a cliff into an abyss. The grief was so intense it felt like my heart was ripped open. I couldn't deal with the world in a logical way. When I was in the grief, in a strange way I wanted to be in it, because it was so real. Anything else would have been a lie. I cried and I wailed and wailed. I didn't know what to do. It was so overwhelming.

The best I could do at that point was to seek out some form of healing. It wasn't even a conscious decision. I was just trying to find things I could resonate with. It was then that I pursued drumming.

Because a friend invited me, I went to a drumming group by chance one evening, and it felt good to hear the drumming even though I was going through the grief. I loved the way it felt to drum. The drum enabled me to express my feelings in a way I couldn't through words. I noticed that whenever I went to a drum circle, when the evening was over, I felt joyful, which was a surprise considering I was in so much grief.

I found that drumming was very healing. It was very primal, and my feelings were also so primal. The drumming was beyond words, beyond images—it was a place of total feeling. I felt at one with everyone I played the drums with. It seemed like a deep inner healing was occurring through my playing the drums.

In this period of my life, I would not miss the drumming for any reason and would go every chance I got because I knew it was a place I could go to get relief from the grief I was experiencing and lose myself. Sometimes when I would go to drumming, I would be upset on the way there, but once there, the rhythm seemed to show me that I could be in the grief and be in the rhythm at the same time.

The rhythm was the best way for me to express the way I felt. Sometimes I felt like I was drumming out my grief. Or I would dance to the rhythm and dance what was going on inside of me. There was no thinking, just completely going with the drumming and letting it take me wherever it would take me. A part of me that had died because of my son's death re-emerged. By the end of the night I would feel amazingly light, like I had released a tremendous amount of emotion. I couldn't believe how light I felt.

The drum seemed to help balance my life and bring me into the present. I also found that my inner child, that part of me that wanted to play, could come out. It was years and years since I felt this wondrous feeling of joy and play that drumming allowed me to feel. Being an adult and making a career starves this inner need for joyful play. I found this to be incredibly healing.

Usually, I am never the one to be in the center of things, yet while drumming, I found myself keeping the beat for the whole group. I felt such a feeling of life and vibrancy while drumming.

I would come back week after week and release and release and feel the same lightness time after time. It was like I began to expect this release through the drum.

There was something about pounding on the drum that helped me to let go of so much grief, anger and rage. The banging and pounding on the drum was my way of crying and screaming out my grief. It was not a conscious process; it was my body releasing. Doing this with a group of people was empowering. I was not alone and it was okay to express whatever I felt. The drumming was a very important key to my healing. Initially it was about a new way for me to move through my grief. As I progressed, I found that I had less and less grief and more and more happiness. Drumming at first was a way to heal my grief, but it became a way to remember my joy.

Tom Dalton, music therapist at Horizons Bereavement Center, a program at Hospice of Palm Beach County, shares his thoughts about drums and emotions.

The drum connects people to what they are feeling and allows them to perhaps move in a new direction. Once they get in touch with a particular emotion, and they are drumming improvisationally, you can see it on their face, that they are moving through their own grief, moving through their sadness and maybe seeing that there is hope, that there is light at the end of this tunnel. They realize, "I won't always feel this sad. Perhaps I will never feel as happy as I did before, but I won't always be in this sad place." That's the great thing about music in general, it allows people to move to different places in real time.

At a recent workshop given for the Board of Education, I gave a group of twenty assistant principals and staff members an opportunity to express their emotions into the drum. I began with a request to have these administrators remember moments when they experienced various emotions and then interpret these emotions as rhythms. One by one, as the emotions were named—fear, sadness, joy and finally, anger—these individuals interpreted their

emotions into various drum beats. Their sadness became low rus-
tling staccato pitter patters. Their happiness involved their bodies
moving to accompany the fast rhythms created by their hands.
Fear elicited tentative spurts. But when I asked them to think of
something that made them angry and then express their anger into
the drum, a woman in the front, who must have had a very recent
experience of anger, began walloping the paddle drum she was playing.

As she turned red with rage, slamming the paddle with seemingly all of her might, individuals behind her began moving away
for their survival as her strokes widened. When the exercise was
completed, she came up to me to let me know she felt much better
than she had in a long time. The drum had enabled her to release
her emotions which were locked within her. Without thinking of
which word would mostly accurately reflect this emotion she was
able to express this feeling and let it go. On the most basic level of
being, she released her anger and emerged relaxed and free.

PART II

Complementary Medicine
and Rhythm

Chapter Five

Drumming and
Physiological Conditions

I regard music therapy as a tool of great power in many neurological disorders–Parkinson's and Alzheimer's–because of its unique capacity to organize or reorganize cerebral function when it has been damaged. –Oliver Sacks, MD

Alzheimer's Disease

As our life spans become longer and longer, mental problems such as Alzheimer's disease and dementia become more common. Many people with these diseases eventually require institutional care. Nursing homes are required to provide activities for residents which enhance the quality of their lives.

Researchers have found that because rhythm is so intrinsic to our nature, Alzheimer's patients, even in the latter stages of the disease, can copy simple rhythms played on a drum. This form of interaction takes on great significance when all other forms of communication have been diminished. Drumming focuses Alzheimer's patients for a short time, and they seem momentarily coherent. These interludes, however brief, are priceless to loved ones.

Barry Bernstein, a registered music therapist from Kansas, is one of the pioneers in researching the effects of rhythm-based music therapy with Alzheimer's patients. In a recent interview, Barry shared these ideas about his work.

I began doing music research in 1988 with Dr. Alicia Clare, a registered music therapist, Director of Music Therapy at the University of Kansas and a research associate at the Colmery-O'Neil Veterans Affairs Medical Center.

At that time nobody had done any research examining the effects of music therapy on this population. We worked with all types of music, but we quickly found that when we provided a rhythmical stimulus, we got the best response. We were able to get the Alzheimer's patients to participate in activities, which to the nursing staff, was amazing.

Typically Alzheimer's patients have a very short attention span. What we found was that over time, the patients remained task-oriented for longer and longer periods of time. By the end of our research, patients were able to participate in activities for 30 minutes (whereas before they were able to stay seated and participate for only a few minutes). This was unheard of. None of the other disciplines in the hospital could involve patients like that. We also received anecdotal reports from the nursing staff that patients were less agitated and had greater eye contact.

The act of drumming provided a potent communication tool, allowing these patients to relate better to their loved ones. We started to develop a process where family members would play drums with their loved ones in order to have a relationship with them. Typically Alzheimer's patients become very withdrawn and disassociative with the world, so it is very painful for family members who want to communicate with a patient who has Alzheimer's. Through drumming, these patients were offered the opportunity to have a relationship and interact with their family, which they were not able to do previously.

In the beginning, the patient would sit in a chair while the family members and I sat along side of them. We would involve the patient in different activities using percussion instruments. All of us would play together. For the family members and the patient to be able to sit, hold each other's hand, make eye contact and play some music allowed the Alzheimer's patient and the family member to get connected to each other. This was a very deep experience for the spouse. We often saw tears of joy at the end of our sessions.

The drum is the most accessible musical instrument, bar none. No other instrument gets people as immediately involved in a successful music making experience as the drum. Through the drum, all kinds of goals can be addressed, be they physical, cognitive or emotional.

We used various kinds of drums, including frame drums and paddle drums. We chose paddle drums because we found that they provided a good source of vibrotactile stimulation. When Alzheimer's patients felt this vibration, their level of participation increased.

We also found that playing with mallets increased their level of participation. Once you play the drums without a mallet, then technique becomes an issue. Once technique becomes an issue, you have something that is a little less accessible. Put a stick in somebody's hand and there is nothing to think about.

We also found that these patients were able to learn rhythm patterns. We would present a rhythm and when they successfully played that twice, we would show them another pattern. In a project that lasted eight weeks, several of the patients were able to learn increasingly complex patterns.

In one of the first research projects using drums with Alzheimer's patients, we demonstrated that late-stage Alzheimer's patients could still learn new skills. We were surprised to find that Alzheimer's patients were able to move their hands to different areas of a hand drum, demonstrating a knowledge of the different regions of the drum.

In my opinion, the reason that rhythm is such a powerful tool is that rhythm accesses the brain globally. For instance vision is in one part of the brain, speech another, but music uses the whole

Barry Bernstein facilitates a drum circle at the Heart of Healing conference attended by psychiatrists, social workers and health care professionals.

brain, so that anything musical can reach the brain through different pathways. In addition, we seem to have a biological need for the structure that rhythm provides. Rhythm helps us organize our reality. Alzheimer's disease disrupts this internal rhythmical processing. The music helps bring it back into the body.

Music therapist Christine Stevens shares her experiences of drumming with Alzheimer's patients.

One of the experiences I had regarding Alzheimer's patients was with a patient who was a restless kind of guy, but he wouldn't leave his room. He was constantly pacing in his room. He would take the sink apart and kind of fix it. He would play with things in there. He was kind of a menace because he would take out his hearing aids and hide them so he actually lost many hearing aids, which are expensive. Finally they just left his hearing aids out. He was, therefore, very hard of hearing. I would go into his room and would bring Remo paddle drums, and we would play together. Initially, he could only sit with me for about five minutes. I would hand him the drum, and I'd hold my drum, and we'd play a little bit together. But within a five minute period, he would put down the drum and start wandering. Starting out, his attention span was very short.

Over the course of about a month, he started being able to sit longer with me. I would reach out and hit his drum, and he'd reach out and hit my drum. So I started doing some interactive stuff, and then one day I went down to his room, and his daughter and her husband were in there visiting. I had these two drums, and they said, "Oh, we'd love to try that." So I went and got two more drums, and then the four of us sat in his room and drummed together, and he really got into it. He was hitting their drums and his drum, and he was changing the rhythms, and he started humming, making up his own music.

This was very exciting to the family, so they decided to keep arranging these visits. Music therapy became the one vehicle where they could interact with him. One of the big goals the recreation staff had for him was to go out of his room and into the day room. So, wanting to work with the goal of social interaction, I talked with his family members, and the family all agreed that we would bring him down into the activity room for drumming sessions.

The four of us sat in the day room and did our drumming together, and as we were drumming along, he started singing "My Bonnie Lies over the Ocean." I looked over and saw that his daughter was crying. He didn't acknowledge that she was crying. He just kept singing. I asked the daughter what the significance of this song was and she said that Bonnie is her sister's name. He named her after that song.

There were two major changes in this Alzheimer's patient. First was the sustaining of an activity, and secondly there was an increase in social interaction. This was a man who was practically deaf. He had no connection to people. He just talked at you. Because of the vibration of the drum, he was able to feel it, thus it created an interaction. He would hit my drum, I would hit his drum. He would hit his daughter's drum and then this would enable him to be brought out into social interaction. The drum seemed to stimulate his memory through singing a song which made sense neurologically. The rhythm helped to create a memory of the song. Not specifically that he thought, "Oh now, I'm thinking of my daughter," but that it brought him to a memory that his family knew was connected to his daughter.

One of the big reasons that drums benefited him was because he was successful at doing it. He could play it, he could participate and begin to know that he was participating with others. I think people don't enjoy being solitary. The drums allowed him to come back into some human connection.

To be more specific, Alzheimer's is a deterioration in the cerebral cortex, and music is processed in many areas of the brain. Therefore, people with Alzheimer's can still participate and cognitively process rhythm. In fact, rhythm is more left hemisphere than right. So if there is somebody with a right hemisphere stroke, and they can't sing melody, they may in fact be perfectly capable of participating in rhythm. But the difference is that the basic rhythm is processed in our cerebellum and that is lower brain stem. So people with Parkinson's (or Alzheimer's), which is a disorder of the basil ganglia, can still participate in rhythm.

One of the things that I loved about Barry Bernstein's research is that the patients improved musically. Now that's fascinating, for someone with Alzheimer's disease to be learning and improving. They were learning with a damaged brain, and yet they didn't remember learning. So there wasn't an integration to the higher cerebral cortex of "Oh I remember you, I remember what we worked on last week." But their playing was improving. So it was like knowing without knowing.

There was another experience of working with Alzheimer's patients. This time I was doing a drumming circle, and I looked over and this woman was taking her mallet and dipping it in her milk to the beat of her music. She was participating, she was creating rhythm by dipping the mallet. Rhythm is so contagious that it effects even the oddest behaviors.

Basic entrainment is stopping and starting together. I remember this one drum circle in an Alzheimer's center. I was a stranger to the facility and a stranger to the patients. I passed out the instruments and got them participating and playing, and I noticed this one woman constantly hitting her drum with no rhythm. She was hitting her drum with only a Parkinson's-like shake. This was the first time that I saw someone not be able to entrain. But then when I said, 4, 3, 2, 1, stop, she stopped.

What was unusual was that she didn't follow the particular beat pattern, but yet what she followed was the overall structure of stopping and starting. So that gave me an appreciation for the rhythm of starting and stopping.

Dr. Connie Tomaino, Director of the Department of Music Therapy, Institute for Music and Neurologic Function, affiliated with Albert Einstein Medical Hospital in Bronx, New York, shares some additional research that has been done with Alzheimer's patients and rhythm.

We did a study that was funded by the New York State Department of Health in 1994 that examined the area of music and memory with people with Alzheimer's disease. Part of that study involved a series of EEGs (brainwaves) in which we compared the changes that occurred before people went into music therapy, midterm, and after they finished the course of therapy, as compared to a control group. During the EEG we presented each person with various types of music. One was a contemporary ballad, one was a Rolling Stone song which was very rhythmic, and lastly, a slow ballad by Frank Sinatra.

What we were looking for was whether there would be any activation of different brain areas. We didn't see any major changes in most of the people, but we did find one area that was most interesting and which seemed significant.

The neurologists found that people who had irregular or weak background brain rhythms became more organized, and the rhythms became more pronounced and higher in frequency when the more rhythmic music was played. We wondered if the rhythms of the music were driving the brain's rhythms to become normalized.

Dr. Oliver Sacks, years ago when he wrote *Awakenings*, gave examples of two Parkinson's patients who had irregular EEGS but which changed when they played the piano or thought about music, so there is an indication that brain rhythms can be stimulated and changed. This kind of information is in the neurological literature all over the place, that is, that brain rhythms are influenced by external rhythms and there is the possibility, then, to influence the brain rhythms through auditory stimuli.

There are several possibilities about the significance of this, such as using this information to help people who can't initiate a movement. It might be possible for someone who has poor short-term memory to then use melodic movement as a cueing device to help them remember some of the information.

Using rhythm, we can relax someone and entrain the body into a more restful state and stimulate parts of the brain that function at those frequencies. Just as we can excite attention through faster rhythms, we can make people very attentive and focused. There are lots of clinical possibilities. Entrainment of brainwaves to external musical rhythms is a very hot topic. Whether it works, though, depends on the person's enjoyment of the music.

I made arrangements through St. Mary's Hospital of New Jersey to provide a drumming program for Alzheimer's patients at a senior care facility. I drove through morning traffic from Queens, New York to Bergen County, New Jersey with paddle drums, shakers, and tambourines in the back seat, and a list of songs tucked safely in my pocket. When I walked into the small activity room I was greeted with twenty patients who sat in a semi-circle. I was happy to see that some of them appeared robust and alert.

I began by removing the instruments from my travel bags as the patients watched my every move. Then as I played a steady, rhythmic drum and beater to the participants while encouraging them to begin drumming themselves. They seemed both fascinated and excited by the intensity of the drumming and most played along rhythmically on their own drums. I walked over to each of them, asked their name, played the rhythm of his or her name and asked them to repeat the rhythm back to me on the drum. This seemed to delight them and many were able to follow this instruction.

I next sang some familiar songs and old favorites with them. I was surprised to see that they sang and drummed to these songs fairly enthusiastically, but nothing prepared me for what was to come.

I had begun to play a calypso beat, when suddenly a jubilant man and a woman with sparkling costume jewelry and a 40's hairstyle sprang up spontaneously and began to ballroom dance with style, grace and perfect rhythm while the others looked on in admiration and drummed for them. The feeling I had was that these dancers were reliving a very positive experience from their pasts.

Catching the dancers' enthusiasm, a distinguished-looking gentleman began to dance a dignified hustle, also right on the beat. One by one, both the patients and staff alike, stood up and rocked, shuffled, and boogied to whatever degree they were able, eyes shining and mouths grinning, including patients whom the staff said were usually very reluctant to participate in any activities. The few who didn't want to dance continued to keep the beat on their drums.

Just as spontaneously as it began, the dancing and drumming found a natural end as we all collapsed in chairs, clapping and laughing in a combination of exhaustion and renewed spirit. Saying a reluctant good-bye, I shook each participant's hand, looked him or her in the eye, and saw a happiness radiating out to me that was all the thanks I needed. At one point, a man kissed my hand as I reached out to shake his, and a woman, in mild stages of Alzheimer's, whispered with an impish grin, "At last they are letting us have some fun!"

During our session, the patients seemed so "normal" that I was slightly taken aback when, in a conversation afterwards with one of the staff, I was reminded that the patients would not remember this experience when I came back the following week. The next week, when I asked some of the patients if they remembered drumming and dancing the week before, they cheerfully replied "No!"

Robert Lawrence Friedman drums with Alzheimer's patients at The Franciscan Home in Jersey City, New Jersey.

Even without their remembering their experience of the prior week, I was happy when it became apparent that their response the second week was even more enthusiastic than the week before.

Cancer

Alan Turry, recently discussed a patient he worked with who had non-Hodgkins Lymphoma:

I worked with an adult client who was diagnosed with non-Hodgkin's lymphoma. She found that moving to rhythms allowed her to get more in touch with her feelings. Though it wasn't specifically rhythmic instruments, she used rhythmic music to help access feelings that she had been repressing. She would come into the session and create a lyric about something that was on her mind. We would then get deeper and deeper into meaningful expression. She would sing about her doctors, the way she felt about herself, the feelings she had. Through moving rhythmically and singing, she would allow herself to connect her ideas to her feelings. At times she would start to cry. Yet she often felt proud of her creation and a sense of relief as she participated in this way. She began to share the music with her friends and family.

She eventually started singing the music to the public. This led to her feeling less isolated and closer to her friends and family. Rhythmic music was a way for her to feel empowered and energized.

Multiple Sclerosis – Two Personal Stories

I asked people in my local drumming community for their experiences in which drumming had had a positive impact on their lives in some way. Surprisingly, the first two stories I received were from women who had suffered from Multiple Sclerosis and been afforded relief from their symptoms after playing the hand drum. Here is the first account as told to me by Melodee Gabler-Tsafas.

Melodee Gabler-Tsafas

The following story is about how being surrounded by the sounds of drumming and by letting myself be open to its healing vibrations, I experienced a profound healing. First I need to give some background to my physical state of health at that time.

I was diagnosed with Multiple Sclerosis April of 1996. The left side of my body was affected. I now understand that what was occurring within my body was really a blockage of energy flow, through my meridians. This condition was created or this dis-ease was due to emotional trauma and stress levels which were extremely high in my life at the time. The symptoms ranged from numbness to tingling all over the body, to hot and cold spots all over the body. Prior to my first drumming experience I had an incredible healing through a Vibrational Healing Musical Workshop. The outcome from this was an amazing healing. My entire body was filled with energy from my chakras being open and allowing the sounds to heal me vibrationally. I recovered full use of my left arm and hand, lost all fatigue and experienced a total shift of consciousness.

The only area of my body which was not healed 100% was my left leg. I had some blockage on my left leg which caused me to have weakness and at times I even dragged my leg a little. It always felt like it was not quite able to move as well as my right leg. My chiropractor recommended coming to a drumming workshop. I had never in my life experienced the incredible energy that exists when you are surrounded by beating rhythms created by many different drummers. I spent four hours listening, drumming along, dancing and just receiving and being open to the energy that was created from the drums. The next morning when I awoke and walked around I was so amazed that my left leg was not blocked anymore! I had total feeling and it seemed normal. I can definitely say that being surrounded by drumming brought me vibrationally in tune with the healing powers within, which we all possess. I feel drumming can facilitate healing for anyone able to be open to receiving.

Here is the second extraordinary story of a woman from my local drumming community who was diagnosed with Multiple Sclerosis and found healing benefits through drumming.

Connie Gulotti

I began hand drumming about two years ago after a trip back from St. Augustine, Florida. While strolling along the Spanish style cobblestone streets and window shopping, my attention was diverted. I heard in the distance a rhythm—a steady pulsating rhythm—I was drawn to it like a magnet. It captivated me and I could not stop walking until I found the source.

The source was around the corner in the middle of a courtyard. A group of "deadheads" had gathered there for a while. They came complete with their brightly colored scarves and headbands, tambourines and even a group mascot—Maxine—a tie-dyed ferret. "The last of the nomads of our culture," I thought to myself as I stood there watching in admiration.

As they danced around in a trance-like state my attention was drawn to a young woman playing a brightly decorated djembe drum (I didn't know what kind of drum it was then). She herself was in a trance-like state and was the keeper of the steady pulsating rhythm. In front of her, at the foot of her drum, stood a giant brass East Indian bowl, filled with money by those who believed in her cause and her rhythm. I carefully dropped my contribution in the bowl as I swayed and moved to the rhythm and secretly wished to someday be part of this in some way.

As I intently watched the young woman I knew the rhythm had drawn her in and taken her to "the zone" (a term I would later come to learn in the drumming circles). I watched for a while, mesmerized. Walking away, I remember the rhythm following me like a shadow, haunting me, luring me, as if not wanting me to leave. And I didn't want to. I could have stayed there forever. I vowed I would find it again somewhere else and have my chance at becoming the keeper of the rhythm.

I was diagnosed with Multiple Sclerosis in 1987. My doctors informed me that it was a chronic progressive neurological illness and that no cure had been found as of present. Medications were available to slow it down somewhat. It scared the heck out of me! I didn't know what to expect day to day. I decided to be my own healer. I lived my life with zest and fervor. I tried to do everything with passion and abandon. Never once considering or caring what others thought. I followed my own calling and my own heart.

I concentrated on the positive things in my life and even decided to have a child, which was quite risky, but worked out well. Friends and family thought I was crazy and had bohemian tendencies. I didn't care. This was where I was most comfortable. This was where I was me. It was a very liberating experience. And I'm glad I decided to start thinking the way I did. As with any chronic illness, you need chronic therapy.

I looked into unconventional treatments and therapies. I took classes in tai-chi, pottery, studied physics and listened to every kind of music from Led Zeppelin to Vivaldi. I watched Marx Brothers movies (which got me through the rough times) and just played and thanked spirit everyday for the goodness in and around me.

One day as I was sitting quietly and reading, I happened to glance over at the pile of magazines and newspapers next to me. I pulled out a spiritually oriented magazine and started reading. I found an article on hand drumming and I froze—there in a distant place in my mind I began to hear the same steady pulsating rhythm I had heard a few years before in St. Augustine. The rhythm had come back.

That Saturday I attended my first drum circle, and I was never the same again. My vow was kept! Among all the other unconventional therapies I have sought, this, by far, has been the most grounding, rewarding, uplifting and enjoyable.

I had been having some problems with weakness and balance along with occasional stiffness. My doctor suggested exercise and medication. I suggested more drumming. I drummed everyday, went to classes and drum circles. The drums have helped my coordination and stiffness as well as my strength. As I attended hand drum classes—both for the conga drum and the djembe drum—my spirit was uplifted and my health improved greatly. I believe drumming is a very personal experience, and we each do it for different reasons but for the same results. The vibrations we make on our drums resonate throughout our bodies, and our cells in turn move to the rhythms we make. When we send these vibrations to our body to heal it or send our vibrations to the world for more love and compassion, the cells remember those vibrations. Just like they remember viruses years later they retain vibrational rhythms and years later something inside you gets stirred up when you hear them or play them. It's all very spiritual, I think. I currently own a djembe drum and a conga drum and drum whenever and wherever I can. Peace to all who drum to send the message of hope and love throughout the world.

Dr. Michael Thaut, Neuroscientist and Director of the Center for Biomedical Research in Music located in Colorado State University, discusses his work with Multiple Sclerosis patients.

We have trained with some Multiple Sclerosis patients, trying to improve their gait. It's a very unpredictable disease and motor functions fluctuate. MS patients who have used this method feel that using this process helps them to walk with more stability, to control their speed and to increase their safety while walking. It is part of the same mechanism, control of timing in their movements, giving a sense of stability. Rhythm is an extremely powerful sensory stimulus that creates some very clear and easily perceivable time structures in the brain. MS patients may be able to lean on that while they try to overcome difficulties in their movements. I absolutely have no doubt of this because of the positive results that patients have reported.

Paralysis

Arthur Hull, a well-known drum circle facilitator, describes an experience involving a woman who used drumming to regain motor function after she was paralyzed.

I did a program in Mill Valley in a hospital once, and a lady came up to me and told me that she had been involved in an accident that paralyzed her. The doctors gave her almost no hope of regaining any movement in her body from her waist down and told her that she had to acknowledge this limitation and live with it. She decided not to. She had upper body movement, and she started playing doumbeks, talking drums and bongos. Because she was a dancer, she didn't think she could live if she couldn't move her legs. She started imagining and moving her body from her prone position, any movement she could manage while she played the drum with her upper torso. She called it "micro muscle movement dancing." Slowly but surely, larger and larger movements occurred to the point that she could wiggle her toes, then move her body, until finally she could sit in a chair and play larger drums. After four years of constant drumming and dancing in this way, she became a dancer again, though now she is a drumming dancer or a dancing drummer depending on her mood. She now has full movement of her body, and she is graceful and beautiful.

Parkinson's Disease

Heather MacTavish

Heather MacTavish, diagnosed with Parkinson's disease in 1995, found the drum instrumental in helping to alleviate the symptoms of her illness. She has now been inspired to facilitate drum circles to help others obtain similar benefits. In this very touching story, she shares her experience.

When I was 46 years old, I was diagnosed with Parkinson's disease. By then, I had been dealing with Parkinson's symptoms for at least five years, and I was not doing well. I owned a book-keeping business and was forced to shut it down because I was no longer able to function well enough to continue my work. My symptoms included loss of balance, inability to write, almost constant pain in my shoulder, arm, back and right leg, dragging my right leg, confusion and memory issues, depression, and hand tremor. My handwriting got smaller until I was often unable to write at all. The stairs to the flat where I lived in San Francisco made normal activities difficult, and I faced the risk and fear of falling.

My neurologist prescribed Sinemet, a drug that replaces the chemical dopamine in the brain. By the time one is diagnosed with Parkinson's disease, it is estimated that 80 percent of the nerve cells in the substantia nigra area of the brain have died, leaving too few remaining to manufacture sufficient quantities of the neurotransmitter dopamine.

Parkinson's disease is similar to Alzheimer's disease in that an absolute diagnosis can only be done on a post-mortem basis. All other possible disorders must be systematically eliminated before a successful response to Sinemet confirms the diagnosis. The Sinemet dosage needed to allow me to function somewhat normally was 12 pills a day.

I moved to Marin County to await the next stage of the disease, expecting that my active and effective life was over. It was a wrenching experience because I had to give up my business, and my business represented my family in a way. My employees were my children, and my clients were my siblings. I felt a huge loss with the move.

I began a regimen that included energy work, meditation, yoga, and exercise and decided to treat myself to something that I had always wanted to do. With no musical background, I bought a harp. I did not understand at the time that the vibrations are effective in much the same way as are those of the drum.

I was introduced to drumming at that time. Initially, I sat in drum circles but could not actively participate because of the pain in my arms. My mobility slowly began to improve, but I had no way of knowing what, in addition to the Sinemet, was responsible for the improvement. I took djembe lessons from Mika Scott in Berkeley. Mika is a talented and compassionate person who is a professional drummer, facilitator, teacher, performer and record-ing artist. His kindness, encouragement and considerable talents were responsible for my initial drum passion.

I was persuaded to have a party for my 50th birthday and invited fifty women, one for each year of my life. A seven hour outdoor ceremony ensued with each woman honoring a special woman in her life. There was a 30-minute drumming circle, facilitated by the extraordinary percussionist Barbara Borden, as well as poetry, song, laughter and tears. The event was patterned from the Kabbalistic teaching that every seventh year should be a year of reflection. The seventh seventh year leads to the Jubilee year, which represents a clearing when one settles debts, frees oneself of old habits and examines one's life. The birthday event turned out to be somewhat of an "alive" wake for me.

About a month after my birthday, I went to a health and healing conference at a local hospital and met Marianne Gontarz York, the innovative Director of Resident services at The Red-woods Retirement Community. Having recently assisted in the hospice care of my best friend who eventually succumbed to cancer, I told Marianne I was interested in volunteering to help residents facing life-threatening illnesses. She had just begun a drumming circle of seniors at The Redwoods and promptly declared that I was to be the drum facilitator.

Having been thrown into the fray, I went to Barbara Borden and asked her to improve my drumming skills and mentor my new drum facilitation endeavor. Barbara soon declared that what I lacked in experience or expertise was made up for by my exuber-ance and attitude. My skills and spirit were enormously boosted last August when I attended Arthur Hull's weeklong Rhythm Playshop in Hawaii. My new life's passion began.

My Parkinson's symptoms have diminished, and I am con-vinced that the drumming is the major factor in my well being. I have not fallen since I began the drumming. Confusion is not as much of an issue and I am currently taking only 2 or 3 Sinemet as opposed to 12 per day. I have added a dopamine booster drug, Mirapex, but have subsequently reduced that dosage as well. My plan is to eventually discontinue all drug therapy and rely solely on the drum's healing benefits.

I believe that the rhythmic nature of the drumbeat has been responsible for my success. I notice that after I facilitate a circle my symptoms are better for a few hours. On days that I do not

Heather MacTavish leads elders from The Redwoods Retirement Community and pre-K children for the 1999 Annual Harvest Drumming Circle in Mill Valley, CA.

drum, my gait difficulties and tremor increase, but don't reach their level of five years ago. With drumming and drum facilitation, even my face looks different. The rigidity has softened dramatically. Just prior to my initial diagnosis, my picture was taken and placed on the face of my credit card. I eventually turned it in and requested one without a picture since most store personnel kept asking me if that was really me. I found that a two-minute trip to the store often took another ten minutes of explanation.

I notice a marked difference in my stride before I walk into a drum circle and after. Although small motor movements in my hand are still challenging (I still have great difficulty writing), my typing has improved. My voice is stronger and I do not choke as often as before. Pain is minimal, providing I do not overuse my arm at the computer or in lugging drums around the county. I still have symptoms, but they are usually manageable unless I am in a high stress situation.

Although Parkinson's disease progresses at varying rates and may stay the same for some time, I don't believe improvement is the norm. My degenerative disease has become a means to a remarkable regeneration of mind, body and spirit.

I now work almost exclusively with others who are physically and developmentally challenged, as well as with the elder population. Thanks to the generosity of my friends and former clients and associates, I have been able to create New Rhythms Foundation. My new life has been a wondrous journey of discovery, and I am grateful. I have received overwhelming support from A (All One Tribe in New Mexico) to Z (Zubin in India). The Foundation currently owns over seventy drums and percussion instruments and now has the first of what promises to become a fleet of "drummobiles," bringing drumming to people at senior long-term care facilities, etc.

Nowadays I listen to and speak with many people facing life-changing events and threatening illnesses and always recommend that they fall in love with something and discover their passion. Mine is drumming and being of service to others, while trusting my fate and enjoying my life enormously.

Dr. Connie Tomaino discusses some of her work with Parkinson's patients and rhythm.

I once worked with a young person with Parkinson's disease who had trouble initiating movement. I explored different rhythm patterns with him. We then made a cassette of different kinds of African drumming that he seemed to find very stimulating and helped him get moving. Anytime he had to walk across a street, whereas in the past he might freeze, he would put on his headphones and listen to African rhythms to get to the other side without freezing in the middle of rush hour traffic. We know that rhythmic cueing works because we have seen it clinically. The underlying mechanisms of how it works is what we are trying to understand better. Freezing in Parkinson's disease is when the person can't initiate movement and literally stops in his or her place. No matter how much he or she tries, he or she can't move. It seems as if the person's will has been removed. Even though the anticipation and desire is there, the patient's body doesn't respond to the signal.

Parkinson's Disease Research

Dr. Michael Thaut

Dr. Michael Thaut is one of the research pioneers in the use of rhythm to enhance the lives of patients with Parkinson's disease, stroke and traumatic brain injury. Dr. Thaut does not use a drum in his work, but rather a metronome or a tape of rhythms. Following is a recent interview with Dr. Thaut.

We study rhythm perception and rhythm production from a neurological point of view. The other area we study is the role of auditory rhythm in the control of movement and applications of rehabilitation to movement disorders, including stroke, Parkinson's and traumatic brain injury.

It has long been known that it is a biological fact that people tend to follow what they hear, which is a form of entrainment. Clinically, entrainment is the frequency of a moving system being determined by the frequency of another moving system. You can observe this when people tap their feet to a strong beat without even noticing it. You can also have entrainment in biological systems on the cellular and molecular level. There is a lot of entrainment in both physical and mechanical phenomena. In my work the auditory rhythm, which could be a metronome, for example, is the entrainer and the patient's motor system is what is being entrained.

Knowledges of the basic physiological sensitivity between the auditory and the motor system is not new, though the exact mechanisms are not entirely known. That is what our research is about.

The process involves looking at how the patients' movements respond to rhythm. They are thus asked to synchronize their movements with the rhythms they hear. We are interested in how a patient's interpretation of what they are hearing rhythmically is integrated into their movements. They will be asked to walk to rhythmic stimuli while we record their movements in a very detailed fashion. We are interested in their muscle activities, the timing of their movements and their gaits. From this information we can generate quite a number of ideas regarding how the auditory and motor system work together.

Then, in terms of our training, the patients use rhythmic stimuli, such as a metronome or musical rhythms as cues to walk to. In other words through entrainment stimuli or frequency cues, they try to synchronize their walking patterns to rhythms and entrain with the rhythms every day for several weeks.

We have done different studies. What we have found is that this work is very successful. The reason that it is so successful is because the theory is based on several components.

Time information in the auditory system is processed very quickly and very accurately. Therefore when a patient listens to auditory time patterns, the auditory system can grab this information and analyze it very quickly, and that helps to create a very stable representation of rhythm in the auditory system. This information is then passed onto the motor system in very early stages of brain processing. The time information from rhythm helps to create temporal structures for the patients' movements. This is especially relevant in patients who have difficulty controlling the timing and the sequencing of movements properly. The task is to synchronize their walking patterns through stepping to rhythms. We ask the patients to walk to the beat of a metronome, for instance, or recorded music. When people walk to a beat the auditory rhythm becomes like a clock, an external time keeper that drives the timing of the patients' movement and creates a structure. Everybody tends to follow the beat patterns when they move. Time seems to play a very essential role in the control of movement.

The auditory rhythm has a very strong entrainment or attractor function to the motor function. Thus, listening to an external source of rhythm helps patients to stabilize all aspects of their movements. By enhancing and stabilizing the timing of the movement, of when to move, sequencing, anticipating and following this kind of external timekeeper all the other aspects of the control of movement in terms of how much muscle force to use, at what point in time to use it, how to sequence movement, how to coordinate movement all fall in place too.

As a therapeutic tool, this process seems to be rather successful for retraining and creating more stable and appropriate walking patterns. This is a model of entrainment of the motor system through the rhythmic time information in the auditory pattern. Through this synchronization process, the external rhythm acts as an external stable time keeper and creates time stability in the motor control systems of the brain and helps them to walk in more stable, faster and more controlled ways.

We are not totally sure where exactly in the brain the auditory information and motor system is. The particular physiological interface in the brain is not from a neuron anatomy. It is probably a multi-center process in terms of subcortical and cortical areas but the basic representation of those time patterns and the sharing or accessing is probably a subcortical process.

We know that from some of the brain imaging studies we have done and from some studies where we have changed some of the timing of the beat patterns at levels below conscious perception that the motor response still follows those kinds of time modulations. In other words, the person may actually not even be aware that his or her finger or hand is moving in time with the beat or is following these subtle changes in time. It seems to be a very basic function that is distributed fairly widely through brain systems, and so it seems to be pretty resilient to injury.

We have seen that recovery of control of movement is possible in Parkinson's and stroke patients and is a huge thing in their lives. If a patient is paralyzed and can't move, and a treatment can help him feel confident to walk from place A to place B, this is a big deal. We have found that Parkinson's patients can overcome freezing through these procedures. This work is contributing to health with people with injuries to the brain in some pretty significant ways.

We have tested patients with Parkinson's disease up to a certain point of severity. We have tested moderate to moderate/severe patients who are still ambulatory, but who have fairly pronounced difficulties with walking. There are later stages in the disease where this type of stimulation is not going to do much because the ambulatory functions are so degraded. There are limits to these kind of facilitation procedures.

Speech Problems

Dr. Connie Tomaino discusses her work with speech-related problems using rhythm.

We did a study that was funded by Haym-Solomon Foundation involving patients with dysarthria. This is a speech problem where the person is able to speak or is cognizant of what words they want to speak but can't coordinate the execution for the speech, so their speech is very garbled. They can't enunciate the actual tones of the words or, like in Parkinson's, their speech is very rushed or jumbled together so there is no clear indication of what the person is trying to say. Breathing and coordination of air movement may also be a problem, so that the person can only say one or two syllables.

Speech therapists have a very specific way of retraining people with this problem to increase the amount of syllables that they can articulate, but there usually is no carryover outside of therapy. What we did in this study and had great success with was to have the patients actually play certain tempos on paddledrums that were similar to the phrases that they needed to learn. As they integrated the pacing and tempo of the phrase, we then embedded the phrase into that rhythm.

For example, if we wanted a patient to learn the phrase, "Today is cold, I need my jacket," they would first play the rhythm on the paddledrum and then speak the phrase in that rhythmic pattern. What we found was, for example, one woman who had cerebral palsy and had a speech problem all her life improved so much that people asked her what had happened. They wondered if she was taking a new medication since her speech improved so much as she got control over her ability to enunciate her words. Working with the paddledrum enabled her to become more aware of the pacing and to integrate the rhythm of speech into her body. It reminded her of what she needed to sound like.

On average we had about 14 people in the study. In the beginning they didn't have more than two or three distinguishable syllables. However, through this work with the drum, they went up as high as 19 distinguishable syllables after three months.

Stroke

Dr. Connie Tomaino, ACTM-BC, shares an experience regarding her work with a stroke patient.

A man who was in our short-term rehabilitation program had a stroke, and he had a left side hemiparesis which means he wasn't paralyzed, but he did lose sensation in the left side of the body. He was in our physical rehabilitation program and was going to be discharged to the community, but he was still shuffling his left leg and literally dragging it. His physical therapist felt he wouldn't be safe walking outside without supervision. The optimal goal for him was to walk independently with a cane. They asked me if there was something we could recommend with music to help him feel his body so he could sway and lift his left side to get a sensation of lifting the leg even though he had limited feeling. I asked his physical therapist to measure his safe walking speed which was the same rhythm as one of Nat King Cole's songs, "Walking My Baby Back Home." I asked him a couple of times a week to walk comfortably to the song, but what he did was interesting. Instead of just walking to it, he did shuffle steps, moving backwards and forwards, almost as if he were dancing.

He said he felt like, in listening to the music, he needed to move more, telling me he hasn't danced since he was a kid. It appeared as if the memory of dancing was still there, and the body wanted to move that way.

In less than two months he was able to lift his leg on the beat, absolutely coordinated in time. In fact, at the end of two months, he actually got the sensation back again so he could again feel the floor. Some might say this is normal recovery, but our guess is that because he was using his leg differently, activating a muscle memory for dancing, there was indication that there is a different motor schemata in the brain for different muscle activity. When you walk you use one, when you dance you use another since it incorporates tempo. Perhaps that kicked in. This is hypothetical. We know clinically that this ability exists. We are trying to prove it scientifically. In this case, the rhythm was more important than the melody, since it was the rhythm at the tempo at which he could walk that initiated the change. The melody helped him sing the song himself and helped him to self-integrate those rhythms.

Chapter Six

Drumming and Psychological Conditions

We are natural timekeepers. That is the irresistibility of music. Music calls to our soul. It calls to places that people have blocked, and sometimes it calls to places that people can't block, and that's why drumming works with addictions patients; it brings them into connection. –Christine Stevens

Addictions

Music therapist and drum circle facilitator Christine Stevens shares her experiences working with hand drums and addictions counseling.

I worked with college-aged, dually diagnosed patients, meaning they have both psychiatric problems and drug addictions. I created a system where we started by jamming with the drums. At first some people didn't want to play, but others would play, and I would tape record them, and we would sit back for ten minutes and listen to the tape.

We would then talk about how our music-playing reflected things that were happening within their group and process the issues that arose. Music helped us discover what the underlying issues were. The bottom line for me is that when people have drug addictions, they are out of human contact. Their love, their relationship, the idealized object is the drug. They are in an object-person relationship, and this is where my psychoanalytic training comes in. The goal is to replace the object of addiction with human relationships.

Group work with addictions is so necessary and healing. At first in the verbal group, they bond through drug stories. In the music group they don't get to talk about that stuff. So what happens is they have the power to play on their own instrument, giving them some boundaries, and yet they connect to the group beat. Because it is irresistible to entrain to the rhythm, they come together. I believe the drumming in addictions work initially pulls the group together, and a group cohesion begins to form.

I have seen this time and time again. I know that even when people refuse to play, that is just their feeling at that moment. It is just that they don't want to be in human contact then. We can process that, we can work on that; we can ask the other people in the group to give feedback. "What is it like not to have this person participate?" "What is your resistance?" It is usually, "I don't want to play an instrument," but we can challenge that.

I think that one of the healing elements of rhythm-based music therapy is the irresistibility of the beat. That is my greatest ally in bringing people into human contact with each other. You can't not fall into the rhythm. It takes a lot more energy not to fall into the rhythm. But some people want to invest that energy because falling into the beat means connecting. It is harder not to fall into the beat because of entrainment. Entrainment is the tendency of people and objects to become synchronized with a dominant rhythm. It is a physics property. The beat corresponds to some internal rhythm that is calling out to it.

We are run by rhythm; our neurons fire at a certain tempo. We are natural timekeepers. That is the irresistibility of music. Music calls to our soul. It calls to places that people have blocked, and sometimes it calls to places that people can't block, and that's why drumming works with addictions patients; it brings them into connection.

Drums are being used to assist individuals who are in drug detoxification programs in dealing with their feelings and releasing their emotions. Tony Scarpa, a music therapist based in New York, recounts his experiences using drums with this population.

I was working with a man in his forties who was a substance abuser but was now in a detoxification program. Everyone in this facility was rehabilitating and detoxing from drug use. He was involved in a weekly group I worked with. This man had been a heavy drug addict and a very tough character. His reaction to coming to a music group was anger and hostility. "What the hell do I have to go to a music group for? What are you crazy?" he said to me. "I don't need to know how to play music, I need to know how to stop my drugs."

He was clearly very resistant to this obviously foreign notion. He reacted this way before coming to group and also when he came to the first group. When I tried to bring him into the group, he came at me with his hostility and anger. He said I was going to waste his time, and I was hurting him because he could be using his time better. "I need something to help me get off these drugs," he argued. Despite his resistance, he did come into the group to try out drumming, but in his words, he would "only do it once."

Everyone had drums, including him, and although he clearly wasn't into it at first, as we began doing various kinds of improvisations with the drums, he seemed to change his attitude. I did a lot of techniques with the drums, for instance everyone plays and stops or one person leads, then the next person leads, then dyads, triads, and whole groups coming together. I did various activities with the drums during the hour and a half session.

When the session finally ended, this man said, "Oh, man that was fantastic. That was the greatest thing I'd ever done. This was great. I'm so glad I came." In fact, his enthusiasm didn't end there. He communicated to people all over the facility telling people how much he loved the experience.

In a detox program, they are in there with 25 strangers. They don't communicate well with each other. They share a room with others. They get into arguments with others about eating, bathing, etc. They usually are very agitated. When you do drugs for 10-20 years and then stop, you become very agitated because you miss that drug. You are having withdrawal, mentally and physically detoxing. You are often mad at the world, and you have 25 people whom you are mad at while they are mad at you. All the while the space is often very limited. For instance I do work in this ward in a hospital, and it isn't a large space. They have a TV set, and they argue over who will watch what.

There is lots of aggravation going on.

Yet at the end of this session, this man was transformed. He was hugging people, saying things like "You are my brother now." There was such a sense of love through the drums. In fact, all the people were communicating by the end of the session.

The difference between the drum group and other groups that were going on is that the others are verbal groups. Verbal groups don't bring people together. There is usually a leader, a psychologist or a rehabilitation counselor in the middle of it, and the patients are around him. The counselor is the first to speak, then each patient tells his or her story, then the next person and the next. The people may comment "I like your story" or "I don't like what you said." But the difference is that one person is talking at a time. What happens in a drum group is that everyone is playing together at the same time. You meld together in love, in ecstasy, through the drum. And you support each other and you work together to build something. When you are drumming you get that euphoria of love of being together.

The improvisations that are filling up the room are like building up a sculpture in the room. If you pull one person out or one rhythm out, the sculpture falls apart. Each person is therefore dependent on the others to create their sound. It's like having cans in a supermarket, if you pull one out of the bottom, all the cans fall. Once a person stops a rhythm, he is missed. There is a feeling of togetherness in the drum group. This man was truly ecstatic, in fact people he hated, he now liked. Drumming brought about a profound transformation for him.

My goals and objectives were reached with this man through the drum. It was through drumming that this patient showed an improved attitude and behavior. The drum improved his social interaction, it promoted self worth, it increased his activities in group, increased his self-expression, increased his reality orientation, and increased his communication.

After the initial session, which was so dramatic, he came to groups once a week for the month he was there. There was a progressive shift. The second time he came, he couldn't wait to get started. During the week he would ask, "When are we having the group again." When it was over, he asked, "When are we going to do this again?" Instead of fighting, he would ask, "What do you want me to carry?" or "Let me help get the people to come in here." He would tell people who came for the first time, "I didn't like it before I started, but you are going to love it, believe me."

The drums let the patients know that they can have a good time with people without their drugs. For drug users, their whole life is about drugs; all of their interactions are about doing drugs with people. Getting together with people without drugs and having fun is a new thing for them. It opens them up to think, "Maybe there are even other ways to have fun besides using drugs with others. Now if there is one way, maybe there are a whole bunch of other ways I haven't looked at." It expanded their ways of thinking.

Increasing social interaction is very important with former drug addicts. In the past the drug caused them to shut themselves off from the world. You want to create social interaction so when they leave they can learn to relate with others in a way other than through using drugs.

You want to increase their communication. The drums allowed them to do that. A lot of these drug users are very young, 13 or 14 when they start using drugs, so their psychological and social growth stopped at that point. When a normal person is 13 or 14, they learn about dates, or going to work and their growth increases. Then they become an adult, and have fun. But a drug user's life stops at 14 or whenever they start using drugs. You are therefore dealing with taking an adult who has to learn life all over again, learn how to socially interact with people, how to communicate with people. These basic lessons have to be learned, including developing feelings of self-worth and self-esteem. Through playing the drum this man was doing something that was building his confidence level. Although this example is very dramatic, using this method has worked for hundreds of my patients.

Disabilities

A life without music can only be seen in black and white. It takes music to add the color. –Artie Shaw

Mr. Alan Turry is co-director of the Nordoff-Robbins Center for Music Therapy and also teaches advanced courses in music therapy at New York University. Recently he spoke about his ideas on rhythm as a therapeutic tool.

> Rhythm is in every kind of music. Even if you eliminate pulse and rhythmic patterns from music, tones themselves create vibration. Though I wouldn't necessarily isolate one aspect of music when working with a client, the rhythmic component is very important. Certainly, in groups, rhythm can be a very important organizing force.
>
> For example, at Bellevue Psychiatric Hospital I worked with severely chronic psychiatric clients. I found that improvised music that was rhythmic was consistently the first port of entry for those patients who, prior to this, were very isolated and often refused to come to morning meetings or even relate to a doctor. These patients were often very hard to reach, but when they heard music that was rhythmic, they would join in.
>
> They seemed to find the rhythms very enticing and a safe way to communicate. The instruments I utilized were often familiar to these clients. I would go on the ward and wheel congas, bongos and other Latin percussion instruments into the room. Some people would come in immediately and begin to improvise rhythmic patterns on the instruments. I would use the guitar to help organize the music by improvising to create musical cohesion among the clients. Other clients who at first refused to participate would enter when they heard the rhythmic music. They were motivated to create rhythmic patterns, which I would try to incorporate into the groups music. Through these experiences, I recognized a number of benefits that rhythm has.
>
> Rhythm creates organization, allowing people to relate to the music without having to relate directly to each other. Through playing rhythms, these patients felt a certain level of safety relating to each other that they wouldn't necessarily feel without the instruments and music. They didn't need to relate to other individuals verbally or deal with interpersonal relationships, and yet they were in an atmosphere of community. This was often the first step to more direct communication and relationship between members, both through musical interaction and through verbal discussion.
>
> In a rhythm ensemble, the beat itself is the driving force. Because everyone is keeping time and following the rhythm, you

don't need to relate directly to another person, for you are relating to the pulse created between people. It's a safe way to begin to feel connected to others. You connect to the pulse, but you don't have to directly negotiate with another being, wondering who's going to talk next, what the next event will be. Feeling the pulse of the music allows you to feel confident of what will happen in the future. You have a sense of security about what's going to happen next. The rhythms have a predictability and continuity about them. The rhythm of the music creates a sense of safety.

I worked with a young man named William who was 30 years old but functioned on the level of a three or four year old. He was very impulsive. He could not sit still and was constantly running around the room. At his initiative (he sat down in front of the snare drum), we began a rhythm ensemble. Ken Aigen, who was the co-therapist, played bass as I continued working on the piano. His drumming in the rhythm ensemble engaged him in a way that nothing else could before. Gradually, the length of time he could stay at the drum increased. He started to improve in other areas as well. His mother could take him to a restaurant for the first time. It seemed like the rhythm engaged the part of him that was 30 years old. He even started to look more mature.

Rhythm does a lot in terms of creating a sense of energy and excitement. Syncopated rhythms, fast tempos can often motivate clients to reach out and engage where previously they did not. I'm thinking of some clients I worked with—two fifteen-year old emotionally disturbed adolescents who were in a catatonic state. People tried different ways of relating to them, talking to them, trying to reach out to them. What helped them finally move out of the catatonic state were the rhythms of rap music. Rap music is a very rhythmic music. Of course, you can argue that they came out of the catatonic state because rap music is something they love, but I think there was also something about the rhythm that allowed them to unfreeze. Rhythm is so much about the body, about being in the body. Before one of these adolescents was able to talk at all in a music therapy group, he could vocalize drum beat rhythms on a microphone. Though he couldn't yet relate to another person, through using rhythm, he was able to take a first step back into the world.

Psychiatric Rehabilitation

Music therapy has been an invaluable tool with many of our
rehabilitation patients. There is no question that the relationship
of music and medicine will blossom because of the advent of
previously unavailable techniques that can now show the effects
of music. —Matthew Lee, Rusk Institute

Jeffrey Longhofer, an anthropologist and Jerry Floersch, a social
worker, and two professional musicians tried an experimental
project, creating a drum ensemble with psychiatric patients from
two Kansas City metropolitan mental health centers, patients with
a spectrum of major mental illnesses, including schizophrenia,
manic depression, and multiple personality disorder, and the results were very positive indeed.

The coordinators of the project did not choose the members of
the ensemble based on ability, or knowledge of drumming or music. In fact, they didn't choose them at all, preferring to accept any
and all would-be drummers who expressed an interest. Attendance
was voluntary, with some patients attending the hour-long drumming sessions only once, others irregularly, while a core group of
ten returned week after week.

The participants were treated as musicians, not patients, and
in the first session were taught a variety of rhythms from the
Dagbamba people of West Africa, based on the concept of the "talking drum." From their work in area high schools, the two professional musicians had developed teaching techniques which enabled
them to teach the beautiful, complex rhythms of the Dagbamba
people quickly and effectively. Within three months, the drumming ensemble was performing at mental health center banquets.
The participants, in the estimation of Longhofer and Floersch, had
benefited greatly from being productive members of a larger group,
something elusive to people with a major mental illness. At the
end of phase one of the project, learning to play the drum rhythms,
the patients were eager to begin phase two, more community con-
certs. Through this experiment, the patients had reached several
goals of psychiatric rehabilitation, such as feeling a sense of accomplishment, developing a skill, contributing to society, and an

increased sense of self-esteem, as indicated by their request to be paid for their performances!

Stress Management

Stress is basically a disconnection from the earth, a forgetting of the breath...It believes that everything is an emergency. Nothing is that important. —Natalie Goldberg

How does the drum help to relieve stress? There are numerous ways this occurs. When people drum, they are generally having fun. It is difficult to be in a playful mode and be stressed at the same time. Also, as described previously, the drum has the capacity to release negative feelings—of which stress is clearly one. When one hits the drum, he or she is placed squarely in the here and now. Some of our stress is created from past or future thoughts of fear, worry, or regret, but it is very difficult to be stressed and be in the present moment.

One of the comments that I hear from participants over and over again is that when they play the drum, they can't hear their thoughts and because they can't hear their thoughts, they remain stress-free. Therefore, when one plays a rhythm, the chatter of the mind is reduced. Thus, another one of the healing aspects of the drum becomes its ability to induce a greater state of inner peace. In addition, drumming increases our Alpha brainwaves, those brainwaves associated with feelings of well-being and euphoria.

In a recent interview, Dr. Barry Quinn, a licensed clinical psychologist, described his results of working with drumming to increase the Alpha brainwaves of his hypervigilant (highly stressed) patients.

What I've found in my clinical work over the past 11 years is that as least 20% of the population does not have Alpha brainwaves. Alpha waves occur when the brain relaxes lightly into an 8 to 12 cycles per second brainwave pattern. Most individuals should be producing this brainwave pattern when they close their eyes and relax their mind. In a thirty minute ideal Transcendental Meditation the brain spends approximately 20 minutes in an Alpha state and 10 minutes in the deeper Theta (4-8 cps) mental state.

There are benefits associated with Alpha waves, such as the ability to relax and keep the mind on idle when it is not focusing on a specific task. Alpha is associated with a general feeling of well-being and euphoria. Individuals who have very high amplitude of Alpha brainwaves have been found to be able to experience more "lucid dreams." People with lower than normal amounts of Alpha or no Alpha have much more mental stress than other people.

There is also a category of people who don't have any Alpha waves and also have low amplitude brainwave activity across all bands. I see this in about 30-40% of the patients I treat. Neurologically, we refer to these people as hypervigilant. The definition of hypervigilance is someone who cannot turn off his or her mental activity for any length of time. They must always be thinking or focusing on something. They tend not to be able to let go of emotional issues but rather obsess relentlessly about them. Many with this brain pattern become alcoholics and highly addicted in a way that makes stopping drinking very difficult for them. It's very hard for them to relax and unwind. Therefore, they generally have a lot of sleep disorders as well. Anything that would increase their Alpha waves would be very beneficial to them.

In pain patients, the amount of Alpha brainwaves a patient has is also an indicator of how well the patient is managing his or her pain. If patients are not managing their pain well, or are overfocused on it, they will lose Alpha waves. On the other hand, if a pain patient is having a good day, the Alpha will go back up.

Until recently, I had never found anything that increased Alpha waves in people that needed most to have more of them, and I am speaking specifically of the hypervigilant population. I tried biofeedback, but it tends only to enhance the Theta waves of relaxation and didn't really affect Alpha much at all. I even had some hypervigilant patients who were transcendental meditators, a group which typically has a higher amplitude of Alpha than the general population, but these hypervigilant meditators had low to non-existent Alpha.

It was suggested to me that I do some research with drums and Alpha waves. What first came to my mind were my hypervigilant patients. Not expecting anything really, I went ahead and took four or five people and did an experiment wherein I got an Alpha wave baseline from them, which was, of course, typically low (below 10 MV) and had them drum for half an hour. The instructions I gave them were to drum a soft slow heartbeat type of rhythm. Not everyone followed the instructions. A couple did some emotional expressive drumming, and one or two might have had too much pain or felt pain from holding the drum due to fibromyalgia, but I found that 50% of the ones I tested got a normal Alpha wave pattern after thirty minutes of drumming, which means that their Alpha waves doubled. They went from 10 microvolts average to 20 microvolts just in the course of one drumming session.

One of the participants was a friend of mine. I had done 15 neurofeedback sessions with him and gotten him into Theta waves but had never been able to get any Alpha waves from him. The drumming was the first and only thing that allowed him to produce Alpha waves. I was quite impressed. I was also impressed by the fact that the Alpha waves occurred in these hypervigilant, high stressed people after only 20-30 minutes. It wasn't after five sessions. It was immediately after the first drumming session.

In another example of the drum's capacity to reduce the effects of stress, Happy Shel, founder of Drums Not Guns, has been testing his blood pressure before and after he plays drums. He shares with us his results.

For the past 3 months, I have been testing the effects of blood pressure through drumming. I use a portable "HealthTeam" Digital Blood Pressure monitor, Model 8100. What I've noticed is that before I go drumming, which is after a busy day of working with insurance clients, my blood pressure will be 128/80; 120/80; 138/98; and somewhere in between. After drumming, my blood pressure is 98/60; 90/48; 88/50. As I am not a doctor, I really can't explain this phenomenon, yet, I know that I am feeling great afterwards. I owe it all to drumming, playing African rhythms.

Chapter Seven

Drumming for
Specific Populations

*There is a place in God's sun for the youth "farthest down" who
has the vision, the determination, and the courage to reach it.
–Mary McLeod Bethune*

At-Risk Adolescents

Drums have been used very successfully with at-risk adolescents in high schools. Recent incidents of violence at numerous high schools around the country illustrate the importance of
teaching anger management to this population. Drums are a very
natural way of helping adolescents deal with anger for a number of
reasons: drumming is a peer-respected activity, drumming is fun,
drumming provides a means of releasing pent-up emotions and
drumming helps to develop a stronger concept of self-worth.

In the Fall of 1994, Kay Sherwood Roskam, Ph.D., a music therapist, took drums to the Harborview Adolescent Center, which treats
young people for a variety of behavioral and psychological difficulties, including physical aggression, psychosis, depression, anxiety,
hyperactivity, acting out and suicidal tendencies. She was both
motivated by the desire to find a musical experience that was good
for teenagers and tired of hearing about how the music many adolescents love, such as Gangsta Rap, Heavy Metal and hip hop can
convey negative ideas that can have a deleterious effect on young
people.

Asking for the toughest, most challenging kids in the facility,
Dr. Roskam was given one girl and four boys, aged fourteen through

sixteen. The girl and one boy dropped out, but three boys completed the program, which consisted of twice-weekly sessions for two semesters, overseen by two student music therapists, the on-site music therapist, and Dr. Roskam herself.

The sessions were balanced between structured and improvisational drumming exercises, though it seemed the improvisational segments provided the most value for the adolescents, giving them a venue for experimenting with issues of power and control, cooperation, and self-expression. Toward the end of the second semester, the boys were delighted when the maker of their drums, Remo Belli, president of Remo, Inc., made a special visit to a session, playing drums with them, infusing them with self-esteem and providing a positive musical role model. After working with the drums, all students made positive behavioral changes and improved dramatically, showing improvements in maturation, self-esteem and positive social interaction.

In retrospect, Dr. Roskam acknowledged that the behavior of the participants was hostile and inappropriate at times, which is natural given their psychological problems, but by the second semester, even the boys themselves were noticing positive changes in their behavior as a result of the drumming program, such as being able to express feelings and better handle their anger.

Dr. Roskam expanded her "music making as therapy" concept to a high school for "at-risk" adolescents in the 1996-1997 school year. The goals of the project were to strengthen the academic performance and psychological well-being of the participants as measured by pre- and post- tests. A second school, which received no music was used as a control group. Participation was voluntary, but only students who fully participated in the program from January 1997 on were considered to be part of the experimental group. Post-test scores indicated some differences in four of nine areas of psychological assessment, including Emotional tone, Overall mental health, Self-confidence and Body image. Students gave positive feedback regarding the project and seventy two percent of teachers and staff reported that the impact on the student's behavior was positive. However, the greatest impact was on student's willingness to participate in groups, with 100% of teachers and staff providing input recognizing strong positive changes in this area.

Arthur Hull shares a story of what happened one day when he worked with at-risk adolescents.

> I was doing a program with gang kids. One of the kids brought a drum with a broken head to me. He said bluntly that before he had drummed that day, he had intended to bust somebody's head and that he didn't care whose head it was. He handed me the broken drum and told me he broke the drum head instead.
>
> What that emphasized to me was what some organizations are using drums for, such as Happy Shel in Dallas who has an organization called "Drums Not Guns." His focus, intention and sensibility is taking percussion instruments into schools and having kids express their frustration through pounding on drums rather than pounding on each other. Because of the universality of that idea, it is applicable to any kids at-risk. Kids who are in kindergarten can get this message. It doesn't matter how old they are.

Drums Not Guns

Drums Not Guns is an organization that was conceived in 1994 to diminish violence among at-risk kids. Drums Not Guns takes drums into the world of youth and uses them as healing tools. Happy Shel, the founder, allows children to beat on drums and release their frustration when they get stressed or angry, rather than hurt themselves or others. Happy also shows the kids he works with how to make and play instruments using junk collected from a recycling center—for example, a water bottle or an empty soap barrel from a car wash to create a drum, or a broom stick to make a shaker stick. He then shows the kids how to play their instrument and create rhythms. He likes to use the heartbeat as a way to demonstrate the rhythms. Happy states that the heartbeat is the number one rhythm. According to Happy,

> [The heartbeat] is the one rhythm crucial to all the healing that goes on. It seems all the rhythms are rooted in the heartbeat, then they go to other places. It keeps us centered and grounded. When the harmonic levels of the drumming get going, everyone gets peaceful, glassy eyed. The rhythms course through each body.

Drums Not Guns has worked with kids from every walk of life—those removed from their homes, those from child protective services, children in church-sponsored homes, kids who are orphans, to name a few. He describes one situation where Drums Not Guns went to a children's museum and drummed with the kids. One of the kids, an 8 year old, followed his group around wanting to help them unload their gear. The child said he never played the drums before. Happy gave him a stick and taught him a simple little beat on the djun-djun. The boy's eyes got big and he said with wonder, "I want to play the drum!" His mother came up and said, "Wow! You really affected my son! He's never wanted to do anything before but watch TV. Where can we get him a drum?" Happy relates another example.

> We did an event last summer in conjunction with an organization doing an international festival. People of different ethnicities came together and exhibited their countries' performing arts. We did the closing ceremony, which was a drum circle. People came from all over the state, at least 300 people. Native Americans in Aztec dress, Saudi Arabians, Iranians, Iraqis, children from Kosovo all started the heartbeat—the little old heartbeat.
>
> This little boy who couldn't speak English came up to me, handed me back the drum and said, "I can't play this. I don't know how." I showed him the heartbeat rhythm, which he heard and started playing. He became more and more joyful as he played this drum. His mother came up to me later and said he hadn't spoken since he had been in America, since they left Kosovo and the bombing had started. She was so awe-struck that we were able to connect to him through a drum and that no one else had been able to speak to him. We like to say that drumming crosses all cultures and language barriers, and this really illustrated it.

In another story regarding drumming with at-risk adolescents, Jim Anderson, a family therapist and drum facilitator, describes his experience at a Probation Placement Center for troubled youth.

> We are finding that by allowing the youth to play drums, we are indirectly encouraging them to hit in a socially appropriate manner. This is a double bind for many of them because they have

*Jim Greiner leads a drum circle benefit
for homeless teens in Santa Cruz, California.*

never been allowed to hit anything before. The rhythm component becomes hypnotizing, while the underlying aggressive
impulses get a chance to be released. This process as sublimation
gives the youth a chance to vent aggressive and hostile impulses
through the drumming, while simultaneously experiencing a
soothing flow of rhythms. The combination of getting out the
anger and the trance-like state helps the child drop his defenses.
Then an experienced therapist like myself can utilize a new frame
of reference through indirect suggestions about how the youth
might experience life and the world around him.

Corporate Employees

*The trouble with corporate America is that too many people with too much
power live in a box (their home) and travel the same road every day to
another box (their office). –Faith Popcorn*

Though stress is prevalent everywhere in our society, it certainly
shows itself in corporate America. Some forward-looking companies are calling upon drum facilitators to help ease the tension, pro-

mote team-building, increase morale and reestablish harmony through the power of the drum. This is well-illustrated in the following stories.

Drumming: Just What The Doctor Ordered – Jim Greiner

"Can you throw enough drums for about 30 people into a suitcase small enough to check onto a plane and immediately fly to San Diego to lead a drum circle for a corporate client? It's an emergency!" Twelve hours later I sat on a plane feeling like Marcus Welby, Drum MD. I had packed fifteen 10" diameter by 2" deep frame drums, ten pairs of maracas, five Ganzas (Brazilian tube shakers), five cowbells with sticks and five pairs of claves (rhythm sticks) plus an extra change of clothing into my largest suitcase and made the next available flight.

This was another first for me. "An emergency!?" I had thought. The management consultant who had called me said there was a manufacturer's Customer Service Department that needed some serious stress releasing, team-building, refocusing work and to have some fun. It seems the manufacturer had done a saturation promotional campaign to the public for a new product before it was ready to ship. Then, glitches in the manufacturing process prevented the product from being ready as promised. Retailers were getting flack from customers who had read about the product but couldn't get it. The retailers were then calling Customer Service and giving them a hard time for not getting the product to them as promised and for advertising it (and cutting into sales of existing products as people waited to buy the "latest, greatest" model) before it was actually ready to sell.

When I arrived in San Diego I was met at the gate, taken to a car and driven directly to the plant. I quietly entered the rear of the multi-use room where the Customer Service staff had gathered. The management consultant was at the other end of the room with someone who was speaking to the group. The group's backs were towards me, but I didn't need to see their faces to read their feelings. Talk about body language! I could feel the physical and mental tension just by looking at their backs. They were like coiled springs, ready to jump if provoked just one more time! They listened but I could tell that they did not hear as the speaker explained, probably not for the first time, what they all had to do to make the situation work for all concerned. He was obviously someone of authority who wanted to make things right for everyone, but the crowd was definitely not on his side.

As the executive spoke it dawned on me that the Customer Service people were probably feeling like they were getting dumped on from the top and all sides; from Management, Marketing, Sales, Production and their customers. Their cubicles were even located on the lowest level of the building, reinforcing the image of being on the bottom of the pile. The consultant had told me that they had been bickering among themselves, so they did not even have the solace of feeling as if they were at the bottom of the pile together!

It was time to drum! The first thing I did was to have them form a line from the front of the room to the rear in order to clear the chairs from the floor to make room for us to stand in a circle. I then put the executive at the end of the line (he thought he was done when he had finished speaking). I told the group, "All right, now it's your turn to pass something on to someone else!" The laughter burst out like steam escaping from a safety valve on a locomotive. They all looked at the executive and saw he was also laughing and they began passing the chairs down the chain to him as he stacked them along the rear wall before leaving the room.

I briefly demonstrated the drums and percussion instruments and the patterns each would play and spoke a little about the importance of everyone playing their parts in order for the rhythm (like any community) to thrive. I knew they had a session scheduled after the drumming to talk with the managers of the other departments about what was on their minds, so I warmed up with some breathing exercises and simple chants to release their vocal inhibitions. I then had them sing their percussion parts before playing them. There is a saying in some drum cultures, "If you can say it, you can play it!" When we sing our parts before playing them we get them into our bodies, where the voice physically lives, and out of our heads, which will only get overwhelmed by trying to keep track of what the hands are doing. This vocalizing also helps us get into the flow state where we are not consciously analyzing what we are doing, but rather operating on an intuitive level, the level that athletes call the Zone.

None of them had ever drummed before. It didn't matter. They drummed now with a passion that quickly brought them together as a team again. They played with each other, to each other and for each other. They danced together, making up unison movements that one person would spontaneously begin but that were immediately taken up by everyone in the group. They wanted to be a team. They needed to trust one another. And they absolutely had to blow off steam! They whooped and hollered, made strange, funny animal sounds to each other and laughed. I loved how they laughed. I saw more than a few glistening eyes as the catharsis of this physical and emotional celebration of coming together as a community grabbed them and shook them out of their dark, inward turning slump.

I left the circle. No one even noticed. The drumming never faltered. It had taken on a life of its own that belonged to this group of people. They didn't need me to tell them about working together. They were playing together, enjoying each other's company, trusting each other to play their part of the rhythm and giving each other the support to try new variations on their parts; to be themselves.

I learned later that their break-out session had gone extremely well. They had spoken with a clarity and a focus, not on blaming other departments, but rather on how they could do their jobs successfully. They talked about their anger and frustration rather than acting out their anger and frustration. And they laughed. And laughed. I think the laughter was as important as the drumming (and I have a very high opinion of the importance of drumming). It is said that laughter is the best medicine. In this particular emergency, laughter, and drumming were just what the doctor ordered.

The Corporate Tribal Meeting

While leading my first drumming workshop at a Fortune 500 corporation in New York, I witnessed for the first time the extraordinary power of rhythm to transform and heal. Fifteen employees were playing hand drums in a semicircle when, without warning, a middle-aged vice president suddenly and spontaneously leapt from his seat. With absolute glee he jumped and danced like a gazelle from one end of the boardroom to the other. The usually sterile room was suddenly transformed into a glorious bridge between the contemporary and the ancient, when celebrations always led to dance. The others remained transfixed in their own rhythms, oblivious to the executive, as if this were a daily occurrence

Robert Lawrence Friedman teaches employees of the Grand
Hyatt Hotel in New York how to drum away stress.

in corporate America.

As the program ended, the participants described their own sense of joy and amazement at their ability to release their stress and pent-up frustrations into their taut-skinned drums.

The drum's ability to provide significant healing only become apparent when I received a call a few days later from the dancing executive. He informed me that his intense chronic back problem of many years had completely disappeared during the workshop. Six months later in a follow-up call, I learned that his back pain had not returned. What medications and modern science could not cure, this ancient healing tool had. Perhaps we will never know what specifically caused this executive's back pain to disappear, yet it was clear that dancing to his rhythm and acting on his joy had miraculously altered his body and set in motion a physiological change that allowed him to be pain-free for the first time in a decade.

This executive's experience became just one of many instances when I had the privilege of watching an individual's ailment naturally disappear through the healing power of the drum.

Arthur Hull shares an experience drumming in corporate America.

I was running a team-building program for a corporation, and the president was participating in the group. There was a certain amount of hierarchy between the business executives and the other people in the circle. Yet I saw something happening to one of the executives in the program.

This executive was going deeper than the metaphor I was presenting, deeper than the socialized team building metaphorical environment. It was starting to affect him physiologically. I saw subtle changes in his body. This guy was expressing things in his physiology, but what clinched it, and this happens often, was that after the program he was waiting in line to thank me.

I was next to the president and all of these guys were thanking me, and this guy was standing back because he was about to cry. He wanted to tell me about this profound thing that happened to him. He was trying to conceal it in this environment. He was an executive at this off-site, and he'd been working together with these guys, and he didn't want them to see him cry.

The president wasn't cooperating; he was hanging out with me, waiting to take me to dinner. I stepped out of the line and walked over to this guy, taking him to a corner. He was about to cry, and I said "I know, I see, I understand." That's all he needed—an acknowledgment of the profound effect of drumming on his being. These kind of experiences occur in all kinds of environments.

Prisoners and Detainees

You can chain me, you can torture me, you can even destroy this body, but you will never imprison my mind. –Mahatma Gandhi

It seems as if there are literally no institutions where the drum cannot provide positive results. In this piece drumming facilitator Jim Greiner shares a very poignant experience he had in one of America's prisons.

Secure and Safe Drumming – Jim Greiner

As I passed through the metal detector on my way to yet another electronically operated door, its solid metal surface broken only by a small, bullet-proof window, I reflected on why I was there. This was not my average corporate or community drumming event. I had been asked to bring drums to this group of prisoners at a San Francisco area County Jail Women's Facility to help them release stress, learn to work with others and have some fun. "But," said the woman who had sat in on one of my drumming events and asked if I would consider volunteering at the jail, "what they also need is to be around a guy who will give them a sense of security and safety, someone whom they can trust." She had talked about the group in general terms, outlining histories of physical and sexual abuse or abandonment by fathers, brothers, other male relatives and friends and lovers and the related drug abuse, prostitution and both minor and serious crimes.

My wife, Evelyn, is a counselor who works with at-risk teens, and she often sees girls who are in the early stages of this kind of unconscionable activity perpetrated by the males who are supposed to be their protectors and mentors, men who should have been positive models for the kinds of men they should have in their lives. The women in this group are the women who were these girls at one time. Instead of growing into strong, proud females who felt part of a nurturing group, and who therefore contributed to their community, they felt alienated, abused, abandoned and, finally, persecuted by a society that did not value them as either women or as members. They had acted out of rage and powerlessness and a sense of desperation and had gotten themselves into this situation.

I had no illusions about turning their lives around in a two-hour drum session. There was nothing I could say to ease the anguish of the young woman there who cradled the battered rag doll as if it were the crack-addicted baby who had been taken from her by the court and placed in a safe foster home. I couldn't erase the hurt, fear and rage of the thirty year old who had been raped by her father for three years from 11 to 14 years old until she ran away to a life of selling her body on the streets. I just wanted to bring them a respite from their daily lives and present a view of life different from that which they had been born into. As we drummed I kept a simple, basic foundation for them as they traveled through the different stages of dealing with their feelings through the drum. I let them drum their anger, then their pain, until we finally got to a place where they could drum together, each adding her own personal story to the rhythms. I started a simple chant that they took up and made their own in a full-voiced gospel that spoke clearly of their power and pride. We drummed together and reached a common ground of cooperation and a brief easing of pain and distrust.

When we took a break I spoke to them about the ideal roles of men and women in communities that valued each person's talents and personalities. I told stories of my visits to small communities in North America, Europe, Africa and the Caribbean and how people who depended upon one another for survival worked together with shared goals in mind rather than with a goal of dominating each other. They seemed especially moved when I spoke about the role of women as both drummers and leaders in ancient Mediterranean cultures. I could see a light go on in their eyes as they considered these new ideas and possibilities. I told them folkloric stories, myths and personal anecdotes about the way different people in both traditional and contemporary societies dealt with the inevitable stresses and disputes inherent in living and working together in a manner that both accepted and valued people's differences.

One of the last things I spoke of was the common goal that both men and women should share of protecting and raising children to take their places in their communities as proud, strong members. None of our eyes were dry as I spoke of the precious beauty, innocence and potential of children and how they deserved to be raised in a safe, secure and loving environment. I then said, gesturing, "Look around you at these walls, locked doors and electronic check points. At least right now you are all safe and secure!" They laughed through their tears.

I then continued, "We have to find a way to make our hearts feel safe and secure in order to renew and nurture the love that lived there as a child, the love that will help us find a rhythm and a power to our lives that will serve us instead of hinder us."

Drumming Detainees

In the Spring of 2000, I had the opportunity to facilitate a drumming program for the detainees at the Hudson County Detention Center in Secaucus, New Jersey. I recall the strange sensation of being patted down for weapons and the surreal experience of waiting for a series of five inch thick doors to open and slam shut as I, accompanied by guards, went deeper into the complex. I worked

*Robert Lawrence Friedman teaches young adults how to drum
away their anger at a drumming workshop at the Hudson County
Detention Center in Secaucus, New Jersey.*

with young men who ranged in age from about 14 to 18 years old
and whose initial attitudes towards the drum ran the gamut from
enthusiastic to shut down and skeptical. I noticed the clear psychological separation between guards and residents and the many
restrictions placed on the latter to ensure that they would not move
beyond their set boundaries.

I was also surprised by the positive feelings I felt for these young
men, for I had been told that some had allegedly committed serious crimes, but looking into their faces, I saw only boys, some feeling the need to display a little bravado, but vulnerable and needy,
nonetheless.

The workshop began and, as always, the drums brought smiles,
focused their attention, and provided a temporary escape from
humdrum reality, but our time together seemed to be over in a
flash. I felt a deep sadness as I prepared to leave them, as if I were
just another adult who was walking out the door abandoning them
to their pain and hopelessness. I didn't know what to say when the
boys asked me when I was coming back, since the two sessions of

my agreement had been completed. However, my most memorable moment was yet to occur when, for a brief shining moment, the walls of this detention center came tumbling down.

On my last visit, as I was packing up, only one young man remained in the room with a guard, waiting for his mother to visit him. (Sadly, he was the only young person who was expecting a visitor during visiting hours that week.) Feeling reluctant to leave, I was compelled to play a few final rhythms on the last djembe to be packed away.

As I hit the drum, the guard seemed to experience what Christine Stevens describes as the "irresistibility of rhythm," for he walked over to the drum, grinned at me, and began hitting the djembe along with me. The young resident, not to be left out, found a space on the drum head for his slender hands and became part of our rhythmic trio. Soon we were wailing on that drum with reckless abandon. Our hands all joined on the drum, and in that moment we all touched a freedom that comes when there are no rules but those that are chosen in a spontaneous rhythmic moment. I glanced at both the young man's face and the guard's, and they both shared the same glowing smile.

As the resident's mother entered the waiting area, we were zapped back to reality. There was a very brief moment of disappointment as we knew the magic had come to an end, though the memory of a prison guard and a detainee drumming as one will remain etched in my mind forever. Once again, through the rhythms of the drum, harmony was created that bridged separate worlds.

Senior Citizens

While we have the gift of life, it seems to me the only tragedy is to allow part of us to die–whether it is our spirit, our creativity or our glorious uniqueness. –Gilda Radner

The drum's ability to create feelings of exhilaration and community make it a natural choice for music therapists and drum facilitators who wish to enhance the lives of those individuals in nursing homes and senior care facilities. In this story drumming facilitator Jim Greiner shares with us a very touching experience in which an elderly woman discovered a new joy—the bongo drum!

Muriel The Bongo Player – Jim Greiner

Muriel was 95 years old when I began leading monthly drumming programs at the retirement community where she lived. The first time I saw her she was being rolled into place in her wheelchair within the circle of about 30 elders. She was very small, under five feet tall and weighed less than 90 pounds. She was slumped over to the right side in her chair, and her hands were curled into a permanent grasping shape by arthritis. Her body looked frail and almost used up. But her eyes! I was immediately struck by their impish sparkle. They were full of life and seemed about to burst out in laughter.

I passed instruments out to each of the members of the circle, putting small congas, ashikos and djembes in front of those who had the physical strength and dexterity to reach and play them, putting frame drums in the laps of those who could play them and giving small maracas and egg shakers to the most frail. I gently placed a small egg shaker in one of Muriel's grasping hands and gave her hand a small squeeze of encouragement. She looked into my eyes and gave me a tiny, beautiful smile that warmed my heart.

I briefly demonstrated the instruments and then led the group in drumming a slow, simple pulse. We sang a few folk songs that everyone knew as we drummed. The group members played their instruments until they got tired; some rested a bit while others drummed, then played again as they were able. Muriel began moving her hand with the egg shaker in a barely perceptible vibration that became larger over the next 15 minutes. She then stopped for a few minutes then began again, this time moving her whole hand and wrist. She lifted her head slightly and looked at the woman on her right side as if seeing her for the first time, exchanged a brief smile and lowered her head again.

Over the course of the next few months Muriel, and the other members of the group, were able to increase their range of physical movements with the instruments and play more compli-cated, interlocking patterns. Their songs became stronger as they found their voices, and their connection to each other grew into a kind of drummer's society within the community. More and more people joined the drumming sessions as word got around about how much fun they were. The Activities Director said the drummers became the liveliest, most social members of the community and constantly invited their friends to join. She also saw growth in their physical movements and their ability to focus.

Muriel most liked the small frame drum and became especially good at getting a clear, melodic tone on it and playing a solid groove. She liked to show me each session how much greater range of movement she had in her fingers, hands and even arms since the previous time. She spoke proudly of how she was reclaiming some of her body from years of inactivity caused by her arthritis.

One day in mid-December, as she was being wheeled into the Activities Room for the drum circle, Muriel seemed to be bursting with extra sparkle and energy. She clearly had something going on that she wanted to tell me about. I sat next to her, and she looked at me with her lively eyes and said, "My great, great grand children visited me yesterday and asked me what I would like for Christmas. Guess what I told them I wanted!" Her whole face lit up with barely contained excitement and humor. "Bongos!" she laughed. "You should have seen the look on their faces!" The pixie in her reveled at the thought of her family's reaction to seeing this new, secret life of hers.

She loved that she could spring such a big surprise on them even at this stage of her life. Muriel got her bongos for Christmas. She told me she played them for her family when she opened the present (without their help, she added proudly). She glowed as she talked of their joy in seeing her play and of how they applauded her when she was done. She loved that they were amazed by her and proud of her. She reveled in giving them pleasure instead of sadness at her frailty.

One day Muriel missed her first drum circle in three years. I immediately knew why. Her gorgeous, pixie spirit had left her aged, frail body. I miss her. I think about her often and I see her sparkling eyes and hear the sweet tone she could get on the frame drum. I laugh as I think about her telling the story of getting the bongos from her astonished family. Thank you Muriel for sharing your joyful spirit with me. Thank you for being in my life.

Vietnam Veterans

War is cruel and you cannot refine it. —William T. Sherman

Dr. John Burt was a Ph.D. faced with a problem. He was a relatively young Quaker, yet he was asked to help Vietnam veterans

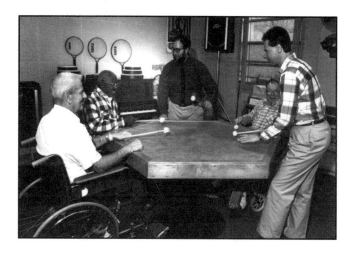

Barry Bernstein (center) with music therapist
Gary Johnson playing the Remo Drum Table.

who were thoroughly traumatized by hellish war experiences, haunted by indescribable horrors, and filled with rage, bitterness and shame. Most were unable to hold a job or maintain a normal family life because of debilitating anxieties, flashbacks and nightmares.

As teenagers fighting in a war, these men had not only faced the threat of their own deaths and the deaths of their friends every moment of every day, but they had also been given the power of life and death over others in a land where it was often impossible to discern friend from foe. It was a kill or be killed environment with rarely an instant to process any of the horror that erupted continually and without warning. These men endured the unimaginable at the behest of their country only to return home and find themselves vilified for their sacrifices, objects of scorn and the embodiment of a nation's division and shame.

When pain is so much a part of a psyche as to be beyond words, what conduit can bridge the hell of the past with the safety of the present and even offer a glimmer of hope for the future? John Burt turned to the drum.

Dr. Burt spoke recently of his experiences working with Vietnam veterans at the National Center for Post-Traumatic Stress Disorder at the VA Medical Center in West Haven, Connecticut.

For the population I worked with, Vietnam veterans with Post-Traumatic Stress Disorder, their aversion to loud sounds attracted me to using the drums. This population has a strong startle response. For instance, if they hear a car backfire, they might hit the ground. Part of the design of the program I was doing was based on the behavioral technique of exposure where if we gradually introduce their most feared stimuli, that is, loud noises, eventually they will learn to discriminate between the sound of a car backfiring and a bomb.

Initially, they were scared as could be seeing the drums. One man pointed to a drum and was just shaking and said, "I will never touch that thing." By the end of the program, he had adopted the smallest drum as his own and was playing it as loudly and confidently as he could.

We would start the program playing the drum very softly. Using the drum as a tool, I was assisting these men in fostering creativity, learning a skill and enhancing communication between each of the members. Drumming gave these men a sense of efficacy, in that they learned a new skill. Most of them had been out of work for a long time and doubted their competence. The whole program inundated them with new skills, so that when they came out they could assimilate more easily into the world. Helping their self-esteem was a major goal, not easily accomplished, but I did have the sense that, by the end of the program, these guys were standing proud and had worked through their shame.

For several weeks, I had them play the drum individually, one person at a time. I didn't want it to get loud until they had gotten used to the sounds of the drum. I would work on dynamics, modulation, feeling the pulse, subdividing the pulse, hearing the different strokes on the drum. At the end of each session, we would process how things had gone.

My favorite thing was having the vets play the heartbeat rhythm together for five to ten minutes because they missed the togetherness that they had in Vietnam. Unifying as a group was the most important metaphor for them. As in Vietnam, they were going through this program as a unit.

One man put his fist through the drum. He wasn't able to modulate the tension level in his body. By hitting his fist through the drum, he had the realization that he can go overboard. My belief is that catharsis is just half of the equation. It's not just the expression of the emotion, but also the restraint of it that is important. You can express an emotion to a degree, but you have to develop restraint. These guys needed to be able to express their emotions, but also restrain them. The moment when they thought they would break the drum, but then backed off, they started to feel in control of their emotions. This guy who hit his fist through the drum started talking about a time when he got angry at his son and put his hand through a wall. His task at this point was to learn to go to the edge of this emotion and then back off. The drumming group helped him practice this vital psychological process.

Dr. Burt found that once the vets began to express and contain their rage using the drums, underlying feelings started to surface—feelings of sadness and despair which finally led to peace.

There was a transition that occurred fairly consistently, that is, the men went from expressing their anger, then expressing their sadness, then expressing their exuberance. Robert Bly said, "The path to joy is through grief." Anger is a defense against grief. After they had expressed their anger, they went into a profound depression as a group. Even in sadness, they were able to express the emotions with the drum, just rubbing the heads of the drum, quietly, slowly, heads down, settling into their grief.

Once a group found their sadness they would go through it and then share, "I am not angry any more." They had to go through the anger and the sadness for the healing to happen. These men have been so angry for so many years because they hadn't allowed themselves to grieve for what happened to them and all of their friends. The drum was able to assist them in that process.

Once the sadness surfaced and was explored, Dr. Burt found that the next stage for the vets was a sense of celebration, joy and even victory. These men had been deprived of any victory celebration upon their homecoming from Vietnam, but now, as a bonded unit, they could play their own victory march.

By the end of the program, one of the most intense things we did was to have them play the drum to imitate the sounds of battle. One person would play the drum as a bomb sound, another as a helicopter, another as a big cannon. Others played the drum imitating different types of machine guns. It got to the point where they tried to come as close to the sound of battle as they could. That was intense. This was the thing that they were most scared of, and they were in control of it. They were making these sounds of battle, and no one was getting hurt.

At the center where Dr. Burt did his work with Vietnam veterans, periodically a different group performs a drum composition, accompanied by an art show and poetry reading. Each man has found his role within the drum ensemble. Whether to lead or follow, add color or provide the steady beat, he is expressing himself in a way that is at once bold and safe.

At the end of the twelve week program, they would invite family members in and read poetry and do a drum performance. They would sit with their drums so proudly. We would create a composition, silence to crescendo to silence. Sometimes some groups liked ending together, filling the room with silence quickly and showing their togetherness. Other times a group would fade out, showing restraint.

Men who fear any kind of closeness have miraculously melded into a unit which has come through the terrifying past into the present moment. Though their drumming tells of pain and struggle, it speaks with a controlled passion, a harnessed power. The men have learned to control their emotional tension and modulate the expression of their feelings. The lessons of the drum will hopefully transfer to their own lives.

Chapter Eight

Drumming and Children

Flowers grow out of dark moments.
–Corita Kent

Healing Children's Grief Through Drumming

When death touches the innocent, their young voices are often silenced by confusion, pain and the intensity of their emotions. The drum has the capacity to speak their inner turmoil and begin the healing process.

In a recent interview, Tom Dalton, music therapist at Horizons Bereavement Center, a program at Hospice of Palm Beach County, shared these thoughts about his work.

As a music therapist, I work with children and teens who have a loved one who has died or is terminally ill. I use music therapy as a modality for providing grief counseling to these children and teenagers. Music, often referred to as a "universal language," can be a less threatening way of working on grief issues than traditional counseling. It's something that children and teens can instantly relate to and can provide a means for developing a therapeutic relationship. Music activities such as singing, songwriting and musical improvisation, are used to help clients express thoughts and feelings about their loss. In that process they are able to explore their own feelings, ask questions about death and dying, and develop ways of coping with life without their loved one.

When first meeting a child or teen who has come for music therapy regarding the death or illness of a loved one, we might explore the different instruments in the music room as a way of establishing rapport. Some of the instruments we have include guitars, keyboards, xylophones and all kinds of percussion instruments, including congas, African talking drums, bongos, paddle drums, maracas, shakers, buffalo drums and electronic percussion. In the process of exploring and playing the different instruments, we are able to talk about what is happening with the person regarding their loved one.

Drumming is a very important part of my work as a music therapist. It offers a way for people, especially children, to express themselves nonverbally. Sometimes it is very overwhelming for a child to lose a parent, grandparent, brother, sister or even a friend. They may have difficulty finding the words to express what they are going through. Playing an instrument, and especially the drums, can offer a way for a child to express the intensity of his or her feelings. The rhythmic aspect of drumming can also offer what we call an "entrainment effect," which I've found often helps children to connect to their physical sensations, emotions and thoughts. In grief work, playing a rhythm on the drum can offer a means for a child to "entrain" to their body, feelings and even their memories of their loved one. It can put them more in touch with a deeper part of themselves and open the door to healing.

As a music therapist, I find that songwriting can be a powerful means for children and teens to express thoughts and feelings about their loved one's death or terminal illness. Within the therapeutic relationship, songwriting can address many grief issues in a creative and unique manner. Music and lyrics are created in a process which allows the child to express many feelings and develop ways of coping with their loss. Songwriting often begins with finding a rhythm on a drum which can express what the person is feeling in that moment. That beat becomes the foundation upon which a song can emerge.

In one experience, I was working with a nine year old boy whose mother had recently died of cancer. We had decided to write a song together about his mom and what he had been feeling about her death. He was having difficulty finding any words to describe what he wanted to say in his song. He seemed overwhelmed with feeling but unable to express it. I suggested maybe we should start with playing instruments. He chose a small hand drum to play and immediately started playing a beat. I matched his drum rhythm playing a guitar accompaniment of chords we randomly selected. As we played this spontaneous music together, he suddenly began to have lyrical ideas and started writing words. His lyrics spoke of how he had never had a chance to say goodbye to his mother before she died. We started to sing his words together in an improvisational melody and as we sang, he began sobbing. The tears that he had kept inside began to come out as we continued to play the song.

This song became a way for him to say goodbye to his mother. His intense feelings of sadness and anger had both a physical and emotional outlet through his drumming. The song had a drum solo in the middle which the boy played with considerable intensity. It "spoke" of the depth of his feelings much more powerfully than just reading the lyrics of his song. In subsequent sessions, many songs emerged which offered opportunities for us to talk about many issues of his mother's death and how he was coping with all the changes in his life. At the core of each songwriting process was the use of drumming as a way of finding a rhythm which represented his own unique grief journey.

I also use drumming as a means of facilitating the expression of anger with children and teens. Feeling angry about a loved one's death is a normal reaction with many young people. Finding a way to express that anger in healthy, appropriate ways is some-times difficult. It is not uncommon for children or teenagers to have problems related to the expression of anger. Some people may get into fights in school, behave aggressively or destroy property, which can lead to more problems. Drumming can be a safe way to express anger. I sometimes offer drumming and drum circles with children and teens in our bereavement support groups as a way of facilitating the expression of anger. Drum circles can also help to create group cohesion and a sense of validation from group members. Knowing that others have similar feelings related to their loss is a very "normalizing" experience for both children and teens.

Drumming and the use of rap music is especially useful in music therapy with teens in bereavement. In working with a 16 year old boy who had lost both of his parents in a car accident, I suggested the idea of creating his own rap music about his experience. While he was very resistant to the idea of "counsel-ing," he liked the thought of creating his own rap music. We used some of the rap beats on an electronic keyboard and added hand percussion, bass and electric guitar. As we created the music, he began to rap "free style," expressing many intense thoughts and emotions regarding his parent's death. His lyrics spoke of how "unfair" it had been and asked "why this happened." He was extremely angry at times, and this anger was expressed by both his lyrics and his drumming. The raps often went into long improvisational drum solos which offered him a means to express and release some of the anger he felt about losing his parents so unexpectedly.

Another great thing about drums is that they are "user friendly." Most people, and especially children, will give them a try without feeling that they have to be musically trained to play them. I also use electronic percussion for clients who want to play different sounds from a synthesizer. In working with a young patient who was dying of AIDS, he had become so weak that he was unable to get out of bed and could barely move his arms or hands. It was also very difficult for him to speak. In previous music therapy sessions, he had enjoyed playing paddle drums and other hand-held percussion. When he became weak in the latter stages of the disease, I began to offer him small, hand-held electronic drum triggers to play. I would place the triggers in his hands, and he played them by simply squeezing. I could adjust the "touch sensitivity" of the triggers so that even as his strength decreased, he was still able to play. This allowed us to continue making music together and enabled him to communicate non-verbally through the electronic drum. We developed a drum code for "yes" (one hit) and "no" (two hits) and continued to create improvisational music together in this manner right up to the time of his death.

The Drum Helps a Distraught Child Choose Life

Sometimes the drum can help a distraught child to choose life. Rob Gottfried, known professionally as "Rob the Drummer," uses a set of drums to impact young adults and children. Rob provides programs to children and young adults based on the drum's ability to create health and wellness. Here Rob recounts his experience at a school in Farmington, Connecticut.

I love working with kids who have the pure energy of reveling in experiences for the first time. On this particular day I worked with middle school-aged children, and I could really feel I was connecting with them. It's a very mysterious process that happens as I allow the drum to be the vehicle for wellness. In my programs, though I play the drum set alone, at the end of my session I always pick several young people to come up and play the drums to experience the drum's ability to change the way they feel through a natural means and to release everything they have stored up inside.

At the end of a session one of the teachers brought back a girl who had played the drums earlier. She was in tears and her teacher asked if I would speak with her.

She was a sullen but beautiful child. She told me that she was going to commit suicide that week and had been very close the night before. She disclosed that her parents were getting a divorce, which for her was somewhat unexpected, and that she was going to have to move to another area losing all of her friends. She told me that playing the drums this day made her feel more alive than she had in months, and that somehow through this experience and my words, she had renewed her faith in life.

As we got up to leave she took an ancient-looking cross that was around her neck and said "I want you to have this. This has been the most special thing I have experienced, and you were there for me today." The sincerity and passionate reality of her gesture so touched me that, from that day, her cross remains on my meditation table. From time to time she has come to some of my programs with one of her parents, so I knew that there was a happy ending.

The drums were a vehicle for this girl that day, as her life changed before my eyes. The drums provided a transformation from death to life, from pain to joy, and yet, I, too, am forever changed by her experience.

Autism

I feel the most important thing in working with autistic kids is to meet them where they are...If I give a child a mallet to play with, and then I match his rhythm, 100% of the time his eyes light up because he gets a sense of what it's like being in rhythm with another human being. –Barry Bernstein, MT-BC

Drumming has been found to be especially effective in working with autistic children, seeming to focus their attention and encourage interaction with others.

Tony Scarpa offers this experience of working with an autistic child.

I worked once a week for a year with a four year old boy who was both autistic and deaf. Originally I had worked with him in a classroom with other children. If you left this child on his own, he would stand in a corner and stim. "Stim" means when an autistic child does something like a repetitive motion, for instance, rocking or making a certain kind of face or moving his or her head back and forth. It is done very fast and hard, and it seems to make the autistic child feel good. Because autistic children have nothing to focus on externally, they stim.

This boy's stim was rocking back and forth in one spot over and over again. With a child like this, because he was so young, if he didn't get enough sensory stimulation, he would get more and more withdrawn from the outside world. And if this isn't corrected when he is young, it is harder to get him to change that behavior and unlearn it when he gets older. If you have a child that is deaf and autistic, it is particularly difficult. The more you can get him to do in terms of relating to the outside world, the better. This child was headed for a group home if his withdrawal continued. The long-term goals would be to get this child to learn to wash his hands, feed himself, play some games, etc.

As a therapist my goal was to find ways to help pull him out of his inner world and take notice of the world around him. We were having lots of difficulty accomplishing that. Since he was deaf, it made it that much harder, since we couldn't speak to him. Being deaf really closed him out, and all they had available was the visual. He could see things going on around him, but since he didn't hear anything, it was as if it was just going on inside of his mind. You couldn't talk to him and say, "Mike, [pseudonym] we are out here, pick up the toy." You couldn't reach him in this way, again, because he couldn't hear.

But when we introduced the drum to him something changed dramatically in him. He could not only see the drum, but feel the vibration of the drum, and through this, realize that there is a person playing it, and realize there is a person talking to him through the drum, trying to reach him, trying to get his attention to look out of his world, and associate that person with the drum.

The fact was that he began to associate my hand with playing the drum since when the sound stopped, my hand stopped playing it, and when the sound started, my hand was hitting the drum. He could see this, and he would respond to it. For instance, when my hand stopped, he would take my hand and try to get me to play by banging my hand on the drum or he would play it himself with his hand. One of my goals was to have him play the drum himself.

In our sessions, he would stand near the drum, with his hands on the top of the conga drum. He was a few inches taller than the drum, and I would play. He would stand there for a half an hour, which was an incredible amount of time for this boy since his attention span when doing anything else was less than a minute.

When he wasn't drumming, he would have a non-expressive look on his face, but when he was drumming, he would come alive. He would start smiling and laughing, jumping all around or dance to the rhythm. He was responding to the drum. He loved feeling the skin and seemingly hearing it through his hands. The moment the drum would start vibrating, he would change immediately. It was almost as if he were in a trance-like state when he wasn't in any activity, but when he started feeling the vibrations of the drum, he would become bright and alert and almost look and act like a normal child.

He was paying attention to the vibrations, which is something he very rarely did. Prior to the drum, nothing would catch his attention, for if he were just looking at something, it wasn't enough to cause him to bring his awareness to it. When feeling the drum, he would often dance when the drumming was playing. This movement would be very different than stimming. The stimming was monotonous, while the dancing was more him lifting his feet to the rhythm, moving his body all around to the beat of the music, wiggling, moving his hand, his head, just like a regular person who was dancing. When the beat would start, he would start; when the beat would stop, he would stop. This really worked for him and nothing else would. If I stopped, he would make a sound, or if I started he would make a sound. When I was drumming he would make sounds, almost like singing.

Before, he didn't realize that there were sounds out there, but with the drum, he realized there was something more and that there were people communicating to him through this sound. He was now aware that there is sound in the world. Before this he couldn't learn to lip read since he didn't associate sound with the world. He didn't know people were trying to reach him. The drum essentially called him out into the world. Once he recognized that someone was out here, he could then progress into better and better communication with others.

The drum had an immediate positive effect on him. There was no warm-up time for him to gain the benefits I mentioned.

Though in the past I would pick up a guitar and sing to him he never responded to that because he was deaf. I brought the drum in and his hand was on it and he immediately jumped out of his world and everyone said "Look, he's moving to the drum!" Everyone got very excited. His social worker saw this, and she was like, "Whoa whoa whoa, he is responding!" Since she was working with him one-on-one, she was very attuned to his needs. Then I started working with him once a week.

The goals and objectives I was able to attain with him through working with this drum included: develop rhythm concepts, improve motor skills, motivate the exploration of the world of sounds and vibrations, enhance communication, develop body image, develop spatial and object concepts, develop imitation skills, develop various affective social and self-help skills, develop verbal skills, improve auditory perception, and develop auditory motor coordination. He would respond to the drum with his voice—that was something he wouldn't do before.

I had the opportunity to work one-on-one with an autistic child after meeting her caregiver/therapist at a local health fair. The caregiver/therapist, Karen, had heard me speak about the power of the drum to provide healthful benefits on a radio station and had also participated in a mini-drumming workshop which I offered at the fair.

Afterwards, she sought me out, and I can only describe her as ebullient at the possibility of someone drumming with her client. We set up an appointment and, though this was my first opportunity working with an autistic child, the session was a total joy. Following is my account after this experience. The names and identities have been altered to protect the privacy of those individuals involved.

I met with Susan, a 10 year old autistic child, for approximately 2 hours. The drumming took place in her therapist's office which is a safe, familiar, and comfortable place for Susan.

I brought a large assortment of musical instruments—hand

drums, pipe drums and shakers—and placed them near Susan, who was sitting on the floor. I wanted to provide Susan with a number of instruments she could play. Instead of using any verbal explanation, I began playing a few of the hand drums and watched Susan's reaction. She seemed delighted at the array of sounds she heard.

Within a very short amount of time, and without any prodding, Susan started drumming and interacting with me—at moments locking into a rhythmic conversation that transcended any words. According to her therapist, Susan had never drummed before, yet she seemed to take very comfortably to the experience. Karen was very surprised that Susan was without the usual reticence and resistance associated with a strange person or an activity initiated by someone else. Susan stayed physically close to me throughout much of her playing, either standing next to me or sitting on a nearby couch.

For long, unbroken stretches of time, Susan and I interacted intensely. Karen shared with me that in the past Susan's attention span was very limited, perhaps three or four minutes at the most, yet Susan remained interested and focused on the drums for almost two hours.

Afterwards Karen said she had never experienced Susan so fully participating through play in a situation that was as social and inclusive as this one. According to Karen, the drum seemed to act as a link, helping to heal the isolation that marked so much of Susan's being-in-her-own world.

The therapist shared that in addition to Susan's heightened sense of social inclusion and participation, she exuded a sense of pride and self-esteem in her handling of the musical instruments. Karen was impressed with Susan's ability to function in such a relaxed and pleasurable way and with the intensity of her focus and concentration.

Though Susan would still take breaks to run to the refrigerator or to the bathroom, for the most part, she was content to stay in the "drumming" room and be a part of the experience. She was allowed time to deal with her upsetting feelings when they surfaced—one time by retreating under the covers on a mat on the floor and another time, drumming out her anger with encouragement from both Karen and myself.

Finally, Susan secluded herself, which I took to be a signal that she'd had enough stimulation and needed to move back into her world.

This session demonstrated to me that drumming can provide a form of personal expression that is natural and comforting and can even bring an autistic child closer to other people and out into the world. Through this experience, I learned that the drum can penetrate the veil of autism that often seems impervious to other forms of contact.

Christine Stevens describes in a recent interview her experience working with the autistic population.

> When I used the drum to work one-on-one with an autistic child, the drum brought the child more into human contact. The biggest difference that I observed was more eye contact. The child was on the conga, and I was on the doumbek, doing call and response. He was able to do the call and response so accurately. His concentration also improved. He was more able to focus. His concentration was there even though his attention-span was short. (He would usually have to go quickly to another instrument.)
>
> I also saw a more regressed autistic child who was fascinated with the cymbal. He would constantly play the cymbal almost to the point of self-stimulation. He wouldn't stop. It's an interesting thing; sometimes they can become obsessive and repetitive with one sound. I had to intervene. I could readjust him on the drum set by joining his beat, and by playing the floor tom-tom until he joined me. None of this was verbal. The only way I could communicate with him was through the drum. That is one of the powers of drumming. Sometimes rhythm is the only way we can communicate with these children.

Barry Bernstein offers his thoughts on his work with autistic children.

> Regarding my work with autistic children, they have a sensitivity to sound and poor social interaction skills. I feel the most important thing in working with autistic kids is to meet them where they are. In their world, they are totally alone. They never

*Christine Stevens provides personal attention at her
drumming event at the 1995 Special Olympics World Games.*

have the experience of being in rhythm with somebody else. If I
say, for example, "John, play this part," I am not giving him the
experience of being with somebody else. But if I give him a mallet
to play with, and then I match his rhythm, 100% of the time his
eyes light up because he gets a sense of what it's like being in
rhythm with another human being. I always start on a purely
improvisational level with my autistic kids. This is one of the
main tenets of Nordoff-Robbins theories, that is, to meet the
client where they are and take them where you want them to go.

Alan Turry, of the Nordoff-Robbins Center for Music Therapy, discusses his work with autistic children.

When we are working with kids who are autistic, rhythmic
patterns can often help them think and have more clarity about
what's going on around them. Kids who are beating in a chaotic
fashion without any organization can suddenly hear a simple
rhythmic pattern, (for instance the quarter half note melodic
rhythm of Jingle Bells) and can begin to organize their own
rhythms and come into a rhythmic relationship with another
person. In this way they are communicating with another person.

There is a relationship between what is going on inside of them and what is happening on the outside, and for an autistic child, that is an accomplishment. Melodic rhythms form in the same way that speech patterns form. Often this can be the first step in developing speech. Speech contains musical components and can be a very effective way of using rhythm in a therapeutic context. By improvising rhythmic patterns from a patient's speech patterns, the therapist can establish initial rapport.

Down Syndrome

Music begins where words end. –Johann Wolfgang Von Goethe

Drumming facilitator Bob Bloom shares his experiences drumming with a woman with Down Syndrome.

I serve as a faculty assistant to Nigerian Master Drummer Babatunde (Baba) Olatunji at two learning centers: The Omega Institute in Rhinebeck, NY, and The Kripalu Institute in Lenox, MA.

In the summer of 1996, a woman named Beth, who was about 50 years old, attended a workshop that Baba was conducting at Omega with her sister, Janine, who was about thirty years old and who has Down Syndrome. Janine was very enthused about drumming and participated very actively in the drumming and dancing of Baba's five-day workshop.

That fall, Baba offered a weekend workshop at Kripalu. Kripalu has a work-study program, which Janine participated in, wherein people with developmental disabilities can hold a salaried job at the facility as cooks, maintenance help, etc. Janine worked in the kitchen, and she also attended the workshop. Beth had purchased an African drum called an "ashiko" for Janine, which she brought to the classes.

Janine lived in a home for women of developmental challenge called Riverbrook in Stockbridge, MA. Due to her excitement about drumming, Janine lobbied to have drumming in the home. The Administrative Director of the facility, Barbara Pastie, contacted an organization "Community Access to the Arts," dedicated to building relationships and providing interactions between artists and those who are physically, mentally and emotionally challenged individuals in the community.

As a result, I was asked to come to the Home to work with Janine and the other residents. About fifteen of the women in the Home became a core group of drummers, and Janine and I worked up three rhythms and songs to perform as a duet. The ensemble performed together in several area grammar schools and at Monument Mountain Regional High School, a facility which has a program for teenage students with special needs. Several of these students joined our core group.

The final performance of the group was given at the studio space of a local artists' gallery. It was attended by the public. In addition to drumming, the group had been training with a movement instructor to choreograph themselves to the live drumming. For several of the rhythms, some of the members danced while the others drummed.

The highlight of the performance was the duet that Janine and I did. She sat next to me in front of the group of community members, teachers, staff, and families, and drummed with high energy and incredible enthusiasm. When the audience applauded in recognition of her playing, she took a graceful bow, and beamed with pride. Her smile lit up the room.

Sandy Newman, Executive Director of Community Access, announced at the performance that it was Janine's diligence and perseverance in bringing drumming to her Home that had led to the performance. Subsequent to the performance, I received a letter from Barbara Pastie, the Administrative Director of the Riverbrook facility. She wrote: "For me, watching Janine perform with you was a reaffirmation of why I choose to work in this field. The highlight of the day was observing how some of the more challenged individuals drummed with gusto and enthusiasm as they became totally engaged in the music. The day was not only fun, but it helped us to achieve our goals of increasing the self-confidence of a diverse and challenged population."

William's Syndrome

Barry Bernstein describes his work with children with William's syndrome, a genetic disorder which causes medical and developmental problems. Across the board he has found drumming to be an accessible tool.

I have found the drum to be a wonderful gateway for unlocking communication and knowledge in children. It is physical, loud and can be very exciting. Many needs can be addressed in this way.

When working with children who have difficulty grasping due to weak muscles, for example, with William's Syndrome, I would put a 22-inch gathering drum in front of them with balls or pennies or squeeze cat toys. When the children hit the drum, these objects bounce up and down, and thus this becomes a game. If I would just give them a mallet, these children would quickly lose interest. Once I put items on the drum, the children can do this for a few minutes. I have the goal of them grasping something, and by exciting and stimulating them with the objects and the drum, the goal is accomplished.

Rhythm Profiles

The founders of the Nordoff-Robbins approach to Creative Music Therapy, Paul Nordoff and Clive Robbins, distilled rhythmic profiles which describe eight categories of rhythmic response patterns that disabled children may exhibit during the course of their music therapy. Through these rhythmic profiles, we can see a child's disability manifest in the way that the child beats a drum, among other areas of rhythmic expression. The categories of response have been developed from observing over 150 children with a wide variety of illnesses. The categories are Complete Rhythmic Freedom, Unstable Rhythmic Freedom, Limited Rhythmic Freedom, Compulsive Beating, Disordered Beating, Evasive Beating, Emotional Force Beating, and Chaotic Creative Beating, and they are described in detail in the text *Therapy in Music for Handicapped Children* by Drs. Nordoff and Robbins.

Dr. Kenneth Aigen, Co-Director of Research for The Nordoff-Robbins Center for Music Therapy at New York University, has worked with children and adults for 20 years as a music therapist. He discusses the use of rhythm at his center.

What we are looking for is how responsive the child can be. If a child shows Complete Rhythmic Freedom, it indicates that the child is able to interact with the music therapist in the context of improvised music. Complete Rhythmic Freedom means having a wide range of expression and responsiveness. If I am playing music with a child and he or she is very responsive to changes in tempo and dynamics, which is loudness or softness, and I can introduce rhythmic patterns, and the child can pick up patterns or play in different key signatures, then that child would be described as having Complete Rhythmic Freedom.

In Unstable Rhythmic Freedom, there is an aspect of freedom in that the child is not bound to any particular tempo, or dynamic level, but often the child will lose control of the tempo or dynamics. For instance, we might engage the child in accelerando, and he or she will reach a certain tempo and then race off. The child seems to become overstimulated and overexcited by the music, indicating an occasional loss of control. There is some freedom in the rhythmic response, but it is limited by the child's losing control. The loss of control can have either psychological or neurological causes.

The third level is Limited Rhythmic Freedom. In this case, there is less of a feel for the music in either a receptive or expressive sense. The child can perceive differences in the music but does not have the coordination to be able to express those changes, and the tempo range in which the child can respond is much more narrow than the first two categories discussed.

The fourth level is Compulsive Beating. It is an inflexible use of tempo and usually is unrelated to what the therapist does even if the therapist plays different time signatures. The quality of beating can be very perseverative, going on and on, seemingly not influenced by anything outside of the child at all.

The fifth level is Disordered Beating. This is more like a discharge of energy and the beating may not be in any particular tempo. Sometimes there might be a lack of coordination, with the child's two hands beating different tempi. When I say beating, a child could be pounding a cluster of keys on a piano because we will use the piano to work with rhythm sometimes, using it as a percussive instrument. In the disordered realm you might have short patterns, but you may not. The child might be able to find certain accents and play them with you and then repeat it.

In general in all of these first four or five levels, there is a willingness, desire and motivation to interact with the music, but at times it may be prevented by either neurological, psychological or motoric impediments.

The sixth pattern is Evasive Beating. In this category, a child will deliberately avoid beating in time to music. The child might drown out the therapist's music or might just keep constantly evading any attempt to match his or her tempo. This could be due to a fear of, or an emotional inability to connect and come into contact with someone else. It is interesting because there are two things going on at once, the child is avoiding emotional contact with the therapist on the one hand, yet by picking up the drum, the child signals a desire for contact. Furthermore, the child must have a high level of awareness and interaction to comprehend the therapist's tempo and take active steps to avoid it. At Nordoff-Robbins, we see this as a very high level of relating because, though the child is resisting emotional contact, he or she is definitely relating to the therapist and reacting strongly in the moment. The relationship between child and therapist can be seen either in its participatory aspects or its resistive aspects; in both cases there is a strong reaction to the therapist's music.

The seventh pattern is Emotional Force Beating. This is not beating to play music, but is more of an energetic discharge, fulfilling an emotional or motoric impulse. The child might ask, "How much noise can I make?" It might be just for fun or perhaps the child just likes making noise. Not all manifestations of the child's playing have a pathological cause.

The final pattern is Chaotic Creative Beating. This is beating that has creative aspects but isn't stable enough to form a basis for relating. It might be connected to the music but in unpredictable ways. There may be moments when we can make rhythmic connections with the child, but as a rule, the rhythms are too chaotic to join with.

The clinical significance of these rhythmic patterns is that the music therapist would see them as the child expressing his or her communicative repertoire in the moment. Autistic children are stereotyped as having an inability to cope with change in their environments. Thus, they need things to be the same, regular and predictable. This need for order can be correlated with an inflexible use of tempo in an improvisational setting. But that doesn't mean that the compulsiveness is a specifically autistic trait because it can also be indicative of a frightened, emotionally disturbed child who sticks to a compulsive tempo because of a feeling that he or she will be overwhelmed by whatever emotions might be released.

Therefore, you can't necessarily use these rhythmic profiles in a diagnostic sense because any given rhythmic profile could have multiple causes. What these rhythmic profiles do is help the therapist to recognize the patients' patterns and grasp the category of response. It enables us to detect organization where otherwise it might be more difficult. In addition, we'll look at these profiles as something not to be extinguished but rather as building blocks for transformation.

For example, let's say a child comes in and plays a steady tempo that is unvarying. We'll initially work with it and try some ways to alter it musically. We might, if one child is playing one steady tempo with no dynamic variation at all, start putting that rhythm into a different time signature and introduce variation into that child's tempo. We're not treating him or her in a behavioral way, trying to extinguish a pathological expression, but we're trying to create a fluid and flexible context around him or her so that the child can gradually transform the response rather than extinguish it.

Through these rhythmic profiles, what we notice is that children who can learn to tolerate novelty and unpredictability in the clinical setting are then better equipped to do so in the external world.

One thing that rhythm really does with a lot of disabled children is it does provide a very strong organizational framework. I think rhythm is most important because of the predictability it provides which establishes a sense of security in children. Because rhythm gives us a predictable element it helps a child and therapist join together.

Part of the goal in music therapy is finding the predictable elements and then varying them. Initially the goal is to create safety, security and a foundation through rhythmic predictability, but then alter it—the child needs a stable environment to help himself to change or grow. Rhythm can provide the musical analog of personal dependability.

The other thing that is really neat is the client's ability to tolerate increasing degrees of unpredictability in the music. One of the goals of improvised music is that it is patterned after normal human interaction. This is a real indicant of clinical growth. Through improvised music, someone in a less threatening way can acclimate to normal human interaction which otherwise can be threatening.

We are not going to take an autistic person and make them not autistic, but what we can do is help them reach their fullest capacity for human experience in the boundaries imposed by their disability.

I'd like to provide you with an example of how we work: a child might walk into a room and pick up a drum stick and start playing something, or might start swaying in a regular rhythm while making non-verbal vocalizations. Our therapists would detect the tonality of the vocalization and start improvising music in that key; the tempo of the physical moments would be taken up in the music. We are creating a musical context around what initially may only be an habitual expression. Our purpose is to develop communication, relationship and intentionality on the child's part through the way that the child's contribution to the music evolves—whether this contribution is through vocalizations, movements, or playing an instrument. The idea is to create a portrait in sound of the client's inner world. Our belief is that this can be perceived by the child, and so an isolated individual then becomes more motivated to interact with the external world.

Rhythm is an essential aspect of this process. Our earliest experiences of safety and security experienced in the womb (mother's breathing and heartbeat) are rhythmic ones. Our developmental milestones all have a rhythmic component as we learn to master different bodily rhythms of tension and release. And so many of the mechanisms of social relating occur through the establishment of shared rhythm. One of the concepts when we are working with a drum is that the child is not beating the drum, the child is playing the music. The child enters into the music in order to participate in the playing of the drum and cymbal because it doesn't require a lot of training, it doesn't need a lot of fine motor skill. There isn't a learning curve before you can jump right in on it.

In therapy, our music therapists have the entire world of music at their disposal. We can play in pentatonic scales, Middle Eastern scales, Spanish scales, whole tone music, classical baroque, romantic style or pop style. For the one particular client mentioned previously, we found that we were using a lot of blues and rock and jazz in his therapy. I was the co-therapist in this situation.

Even though I was the assistant therapist in this case, I began playing music as well, and we almost formed a trio. The client would play the drums, the primary therapist would play the piano and I would play the bass guitar. We were able to establish very unique communal feelings through using blues music.

What I've been looking at is what anthropologists talk about as "communitas." There is another concept I have to introduce before I describe communitas, and that is what anthropologists call "liminality." Liminality is the transitional time period between the states mediated by rites of passage. So for example if a person is moving from adolescence to adulthood, that transition time is called liminality. What anthropologists call "communitas" is a "feeling engendered in people who experience this liminal state together." When you experience this liminal state together you develop these feelings of communitas. Therefore, when people go through certain rites of passage together they begin to have an experience of one another outside of their roles and make the transition from one state of life to another.

The process of music therapy can then be seen as a transition ritual. Adolescents form different subgroups and subcultures; they have their own rules, and they create certain rites of passage that allow them to enter adulthood.

Handicapped individuals are often denied access to social structures, arts and politics, things that could enable them to create their own rites of passage and move to the next developmental stage of life. What we're finding is particularly through the rhythm element of music, when it uses musical idioms as utilized in dance styles, that we are able to create these very powerful communal feelings which then can provide a substitute for the disabled person who has the same needs for rites of passage as we all do, but doesn't have any access to them because of his or her disability. We feel that one of the most important ways we use rhythm in our work is creating these feelings of communitas.

Rhythm can change our experience of time into what anthropologists sometimes call "sacred time." Rhythm can help elevate us out of profane time into sacred time. It's within sacred time that change can happen.

Chapter Nine

Skeptics and Visionaries

Counterpoint

Though my bias must be quite clear by now, I feel that this book would not be complete if I did not offer a counterpoint to the many benefits of drumming already discussed. There are a few contraindications regarding drumming that I am aware of, though there may be others of which I am not cognizant.

Though drumming can be a vital tool for providing health benefits, as so many researchers have attested, and is, in my opinion a burgeoning science awaiting more research, as with anything positive, there are possible negatives.

On the most basic level, drumming is a physical activity and, though it can be quite relaxing when played slowly, when played at fast tempos, it can truly get the heart racing. As with any physical activity, if you plan on drumming at fast tempos, it is suggested that you have your heart and general physical condition checked by a medical doctor.

Also, as with any stress management vehicle, drumming can lower one's blood pressure, as we learned from Happy Shel. Therefore, if you are taking medication to lower your blood pressure, you should speak to your physician to see if there are any dangers.

Dr. Quinn's following account of a Vietnam veteran who spontaneously entrained to drumming rhythms illustrates that with certain populations and under certain conditions, drumming can produce unexpected reactions.

I was at a yoga conference in which a group was doing some very fast drumming—four beats per second. There was a Vietnam vet present who was not drumming, only listening. He immediately was entrained by the beat and went into a sort of a trance or perhaps flashback. The people from the conference gently brought him out of it, but the entrainment of the sound pulsating at four beats per second took him into some type of altered state.

Four beats per second is a Theta rhythm entrainment. When you go into theta, you are going into a hypnotic state, and for people with Post-Traumatic Stress Disorder, that is often when they will have an abreaction of a traumatic memory.

Due to the possibility of drumming inducing a trance-like state, those individuals who may have deep repressed emotions could experience a negative reaction while drumming or listening to the drum. Though the possibility of this occurring is rather remote, if you are someone with, for example, Post-Traumatic Stress Disorder, you might want to consult with a professional, either a therapist or music therapist, who can provide a safe passage through these feelings.

Furthermore, as pointed out to me by Alan Turrey, sometimes drumming can be used as an escape from relationships and/or the emotions connected with them. Since the drum can induce trance, an individual and/or group may choose to escape from a negative emotion and/or relationship within the group, rather than face them. Alan Turrey, stated the following in a recent interview.

An example of an abreaction to drumming would be if there is a conflict between two people, instead of them dealing directly with the issues, the clients may decide to trance out together using the drum as a way of avoiding their conflict. Though sometimes that kind of shared experience can create support and alliance which could make working through conflict easier, nevertheless it is the job of the therapist to discern what is important for those clients. For instance, are the group members at a stage where drumming to create trance is an important development for these individuals or is it a way of the these clients avoiding dealing with their feelings rather than being more authentic?

Finally, though we have heard from a number of music therapists about positive reactions of autistic children to drumming, there
is additional data that suggests that autistic children can be overstimulated by drumming and perhaps also have a negative reaction to very high pitched sounds. Thus, it is important to be aware
of how rhythms might affect different populations. Drumming may
not be for everyone. I believe it can be of great benefit to a great
many people, but its limits must also be recognized.

Visionaries and Rhythm

How rhythm and drumming is used in the future will be determined by the visionaries among us. Dr. Connie Tomaino shares a
few experiences she has had with various inventors and their cre-
ations.

> There is a company in California called Wave Access where
> Jonathan Purcell developed a software program called Wave
> Rider that uses EMG, signals from the muscles, and EEG, signals
> from the brain, to serve as midi triggers for sound. The program
> basically converts these electrical body signals into digital signals.
> We used the EMG device as a way to get people who are recover-
> ing from stroke to become aware of how their muscles are moving
> in various muscle groups. We arranged for a percussion sound to
> be triggered every time the muscle group got activated, for
> instance, the flexor digitalis muscle in the forearm.
>   There was one woman who had a lot of weakness and a resting
> tremor in her muscles. She had no control over it. Because this
> device is similar to biofeedback, the more she moved the target
> muscles, the more the sound increased. For example, this woman
> was asked to make a fist and release it. The motion of making a
> fist caused the drum sound to increase. When she opened her
> hand and rested the sound stopped. What happened was that as
> she became more conscious of what she was doing because of the
> drum sound, she actually lost the resting tremor.
>   Because we had a graph of the EMG signal, we could actually

see a flat line, whereas before we could see peaks because of her tremor. This is one example of how you can use the body's electrical rhythms to trigger a musical interface that can then give feedback to the person.

In addition, there is a new device being explored by Charles Butler, MD, who is on the board of our Institute. He is a medical doctor and cardiothoracic surgery with a Ph.D. in biophysics.

You can't talk about rhythm without discussing the inherent frequencies of the body. This doctor has been exploring the use of physioacoustics. He found that certain frequencies may inhibit the body from experiencing pain.

He did a preliminary study with cardiothoracic patients after surgery. The signal from this device was embedded in an air mattress that the patient rested on after surgery. The mattress itself doesn't vibrate, but the device transmits a frequency of 40 hertz, determined to be the frequency at which the major muscle groups of the back vibrate. When these muscle groups were externally vibrated by this device at that particular frequency, the patients often reported that they felt less pain.

In his small sample, he had people who left the hospital five days early due to this device. They were out of bed the night of surgery and went from a hospital cost of $40-$50,000 per patient to $17,000 per patient because they didn't need morphine and an extended hospital stay after surgery.

When Eastern practitioners talk about chakras, they are referring to different organs of the body vibrating at different frequencies. Scientific evidence shows that certain parts of the body do vibrate spontaneously at certain frequencies which may allow for the experience of pain relief. Studies along these lines haven't been out that long since this technology is brand new.

The main reason rhythm seems to work is that we are so responsive to sound. Because of the way our bodies both viscerally and neurologically process sound, we have a way of tapping into natural mechanisms of the body that are available to all of us. These methods allow individuals who have lost some mechanisms due to neurologic illness to regain some functioning. The most significant benefit is to have a way to bypass a damaged area and use the body's inherent rhythmicity to help regain some function. Neuroscience is just at the brink of being able to show how this occurs due to new technologies.

Physioacoustics

As Connie Tomaino stated previously, it is difficult to speak of rhythm without discussing sound frequency. For the last ten years, Dr. Charles F. Butler, a Board Certified Cardiac Surgeon with a Ph.D. in Biophysics, has written several books, multiple book chapters and thirty scientific papers on various scientific subjects. Most of his research and writings have been on the effects of low frequency sound on human beings.

Dr. Charles Butler, in a recent interview, shares his work with low frequency sound.

If you look back historically, low frequency sound has been used from ancient times. Its use by the Australian Aborigines, the chanting of Tibetan Monks, and perhaps even Gregorian Chant form examples of sound used to obtain the physiologic effects of calming and stress reduction. Anything more than cursory observation makes it clear that certain frequencies and rhythms can be used in different ways to calm or excite, to affect muscle tone or even blood pressure.

We all stand, as Newton said, on the shoulders of the giants who went before us. The first case study on the effects of low frequency sound on human beings was first done by a German psychiatrist named Teirich (1959). Teirich had a patient, Parson Sutermeister who lost his hearing and speech after a bout of meningitis. Sutermeister became extremely depressed and withdrawn. Teirich put large speakers into a couch to transmit the vibratory aspects of music directly into the back of the patient. Sutermeister learned to appreciate music not as Helen Keller did (through the fingers) but by using his back as a receiving station. Sutermeister's melancholy disposition went away. He became a regular concertgoer. Once again he took joy in life. He describes his experience— "My main receiving station is my back. The sound penetrates here and flows through the whole trunk of my body which feels like a hollow vessel struck rhythmically, resounding now louder, now softer, dependent on the intensity of the music. But there is not the slightest sensation in my head and hands—the head is least sensitive." Teirich discovered that by using bass sounds, his patient was able to feel the vibration of the music. His body became a receiving station and through this, Parson Sutermeister got over his depression.

In 1982, Olav Skille, from Norway, described his work with disturbed children. He took speakers and pressed them against a large beanbag chair. He put the disturbed children on this chair. When he played bass sounds, the children would relax. Even if they had been aggressive before, they would become peaceful. Olav spent years studying how different frequencies affected the human body. Most of us who work with low frequency sound work in the range of 20-120 hertz. We distinguish between infrasound (below 20 hertz) and low frequency sound (20 to 120 hertz). Infrasound as demonstrated by Forsvatets Materielverk of the Swedish Defense Administration has many bad side effects. For example, 4 hertz will cause a person to lose hand-eye coordination, 5 hertz creates nausea and motion sickness, and 6 hertz is harmful to vertebral bodies. Low frequency sine waves in the range of 20 to 120 hertz do not appear to be harmful. In fact they are at the lowest based range of human hearing. For example, the lowest key on the piano is 18.5 hertz. Many frequencies in this range appear to elicit the favorable physiologic effects first observed by Teirich, Skille and Lehikoinen.

As Skille's work continued, he fixed speakers under a bed, then had people lie on it. He would then use his sine wave generator to gradually increase sound from 20 hertz upward and asked the patient to describe the sensation. The feeling one has lying on one of these beds is incredible! You feel sensations in different parts of your body depending on what the sine wave frequency is. The bed when tuned to a frequency felt directly in the area of muscle or skeletal pain would often cure the patient of that pain. For example, a patient might come in with a sore arm. The therapist might tune the sine wave generator until a frequency was determined which was perceived in the area of pain. The therapist would then determine what kind of music the patient liked. As the patient lay on the bed listening to the chosen music, the low frequency tone would be mixed in the music coming from the speakers attached to the bottom of the bed. The low-frequency sound waves would cause the patient's pain to disappear.

Almost simultaneously, Petri Lehikoinen from the Sibelius Academy in Finland realized that while a specific frequency might cure a specific ailment at a specific time, the same frequency might not always be felt in exactly the same place. Small variations in tuning would be necessary to repeatedly affect the same location. It was his genius that led to the development of Physioacoustics, a system more advanced than that devised by Skille in that a computerized program was used to vary frequencies slightly through ranges necessary to obtain a repeatable desired effect on any number of patients without constantly reprogramming. In our current use of sound wave generation, we use Petri Lehikoinen's computerized sine wave frequency scanning programs for different ailments and conditions. The author has used this device to good effect on cardiac surgery patients.

In the early 1990's, a Roundtable on Excellence in Cardiology was established to cut down on the length of time patients spent in the hospital when undergoing cardiac surgery. They suggested using very short-acting anesthetics with "voice control" of pain. When the patient awakens on a ventilator, his nurse tries to give him assurance that he is okay. She may tell him that others in the same situation use little in the way of pain medication. She may offer him pain medication with the reminder that if he accepts it, his time on the ventilator may be extended.

It seemed that it would be a lot better if a low-frequency sound program could be devised to alleviate the patient's pain and anxiety. Such a program would allow the patient to receive "physioacoustic" treatment on a demand basis. The patient could also receive conventional pain medicine whenever desired without the psychological pressure of "voice control anesthesia." Under the circumstances it was hoped that the patient might use less narcotic because less was needed, rather than because of social pressure.

This experiment was carried out using a "physioacoustic" program with frequencies suited to relaxation and anxiety relief combined with frequencies that were known to relax the major muscles of the back. After surgery patients were given two control buttons. One would activate the low-frequency sound program. The other would automatically infuse morphine intravenously. Patients were allowed to push the buttons at will.

Many patients repeatedly chose the sound program and used little narcotic. The sound waves appeared to relieve their pain/anxiety, allowing them to rest comfortably without the undesirable side effects of sedation. During this period the average time on the ventilator after heart surgery decreased from seventeen to seven hours. The time in the Cardiac Surgery Unit was reduced from two days to one day. Time in the hospital was reduced from nine to four and a half days. We attribute these changes to decreased sedation and the early mobilization, which this makes possible.

This phenomenon could have many important ramifications. Two of the leading causes of death after major surgery are pneumonia and blood clots to the lungs. If we can decrease the ventilator time, we should logically decrease the instance of pneumonia. It is commonly accepted that fatal blood clots form in the legs of bedridden patients. Early mobilization should decrease the problem. In short, it was energizing to the surgical team to see an occasional patient who was operated on the morning sitting by his bedside reading a newspaper in the evening, and it was energizing to the hospital administration to see the cost of cardiac surgery decrease from $55,000 to $17,000 per case.

Martha Burke has carried out several studies using both physioacoustic therapy and music. Two pilot studies were performed at Duke University Medical Center. The first study showed that total knee replacement patients receiving physioacoustic therapy and music prior to and during physical therapy sessions accomplished greater range of motion and reported less pain at the completion of the sessions than those receiving standard care. A second study in which physioacoustic therapy and music were incorporated into the surgery experience showed that patients who received music/physioacoustic therapy were more satisfied with their care, felt their pain was better controlled, and were statistically significantly less anxious both prior to entering the operating room and again on the second post-operative day than those receiving standard care.

The National Cancer Institute funded the Center for Music Therapy Research, under the direction of Martha Burke, to evaluate the effects of physioacoustic therapy on pain management for cancer patients at the end of life. A randomized controlled study was carried out at Triangle Hospice of Duke University. Subjects ($N=25$) were given three 20-minute vibration sessions a day during a 48-hour period. Medication data showed that subjects in the vibration group used an average daily equianalgesic dose of 51 mg morphine sulphate (IM/IV) compared with 181 mg in the conventional therapy group (p = .06). Although these findings are encouraging, this study needs to be carried out with a much larger sample. A multicenter study involving home care is now planned for this population.

Currently, there is a study in progress at the National Institute of Health to determine possible beneficial effects of low frequency sound on postoperative patients and their immune systems. Positive findings here would be exciting. It could play an important role in patients' recovery after cancer surgery. Even after successful cancer surgery, there are some cancer cells left in the body. Long-term survival or recurrence of disease depends upon the immune system's ability to destroy these microscopic cells. The stress of the surgery weakens the body's immune system. Using low frequency sound waves, European researchers have demonstrated the ability to decrease stress and lower steroid hormone levels. Confirmation of these findings in the NIH study could put us onto a new track that might increase long-term survival in cancer surgery patients by the use of sound! The therapeutic use of sound is fascinating. We are just working through what it can and cannot do.

Dr. Petri Lehikoinen, a neurophysiologist in Finland, used similar sounds and tones though a stronger and more rhythmic excitation program with three ski jumpers at the Lillehammer Olympics. One of the problems ski jumpers face is the long wait between jumps. Low frequency sound waves were used to relax them after they jumped and then to excite their muscles right before they had to jump again. The three athletes he treated won the gold, silver and bronze medals.

Dr. Tony Wigram, president of the World Federation of Music Therapy and Head of Doctoral studies at the University of Aalborg (Denmark) used low frequency sound on children with spastic limbs, that is, limbs with limited range of motion. He would have a physiotherapist measure the mobility of the joints of each child before and after a session in which the child would either be exposed to music or music and low frequency sound. After each treatment session the physiotherapist would again measure joint motion. The physiotherapist did not know which treatment each child received. The children who were exposed to music alone were unchanged while those exposed to music plus low frequency sound showed significant increase in range of motion. Dr. Wigram did another study on low frequency sound versus physiotherapy in the same group of children. Physiotherapy is excellent for increasing mobility in spastic joints. It is unfortunately labor-intensive and expensive. This means that most patients would be unlikely to receive more than a few treatments a week. A physioacoustic treatment could be administered with the touch of a button by a caregiver, allowing more numerous and less expensive treatments. Dr. Wigram discovered that low frequency sound alone gave as much improvement in joint motion as a full physiotherapy session.

Dr. Petri Lehikoinen used daily physioacoustic therapy on two young women, one twelve years of age, the other twenty-three. Both had severe neurologic diseases that left their bodies severely contracted in what might resemble the "fetal position." Both of these young women were judged to be at the end of their lives. No further medical treatment was to be given to them. At the parents' request, each of these young women were exposed to 20 minutes a day of physioacoustic treatment. Over four months both young women demonstrated remarkable improvement, being able to move their limbs, and progressed from bedridden to wheelchair status. Dr. Lehikoinen documented both of these remarkable cases on time-lapse video!

The Finnish socialized health care system pays for physioacoustic therapy in multiply handicapped, autistic, and brain trauma patients. They also offer reimbursement for physioacoustic therapy for psychiatric and drug abuse treatment. The Government of Finland believes that there is a substantial body of knowledge in their national experience that this treatment improves learning ability in the impaired and helps all of these groups recover more quickly both physically and mentally.

This is a new field. Researchers are still scratching the surface of the physiology of sound. Low frequency sound doesn't have the side effects of prescription medicine. It holds promise of a whole new treatment methodology. It is now time for competent scientists and clinicians to define both its uses and its limitations.

Physioacoustic equipment is not yet available for general sale in United States (as of September, 2000). It is currently available for selected research projects and in some special circumstances. It will be available to the general public as research in the United States progresses.

The Future of Drumming

As our Western culture is in the process of developing its own rhythmaculture, it is also in the process of discovering the drum and rhythm as a tool for healing. —Arthur Hull

Barry Bernstein shares his thoughts on the future of drumming in the 21st century.

I resonate with Babatunde Olatunji's wish for the next century, "To Have a Drum in Every House." For better or worse, we have chosen the nuclear family unit as the basis of our culture, and most families are not connecting; everyone is too busy. Many of the problems families are experiencing right now could be addressed by simply staying home, turning off the TV and playing music together, even once a week. It would give families an opportunity to get out of the box of their daily grind. Parents would see their kids as creative expressive beings.

In the last century we distanced ourselves from nature. As this happens we can feel ungrounded, isolated and unconnected to others. The drum creates community. The drum is community. We are all craving this type of connection. It is a biological need. I feel we are being given a gift, a reminder so to speak, that rhythm heals. My wish is that this gift will be celebrated in all walks of life, that children would come together in the gym and so do some kind of rhythm-based practice together, connecting their bodies, hearts and souls. Imagine going to work and starting your day by playing music with your office mates…By vibrating together, we open the door to possibility. The door has been opened!

An Ancient Healing Instrument Meets the Future

The following fantasy represents a world not too far in the distant future.

After a long hard day at work you come home exhausted and stressed. You glance at your television and let out a deep sigh. You think about what may be on television, th news, too depressing, a television sitcom, too predictable. You already know that television will not really help you—perhaps distract you, at best. You walk into your den, glancing up at a shelf filled with your drums, a djembe you use for fun and exhilaration, a hoop drum you use for placing yourself into a deep trance state, and an Ashiko drum you use when you can't decide between the two.

You decide on the Buffalo drum. With one hand holding the drum and the other one holding the mallet, you close your eyes, sitting comfortably in your cushioned chair. The only thing on your mind now is the thought of using this drum to put yourself into a deep and relaxing state of mind.

You take a deep breath in and settle into the back of the chair. You let out a sigh and feel the relaxation moving throughout your body, in anticipation of this extraordinary experience.

Slowly and deliberately you begin to strike the drum with the mallet, each beat coinciding with a breath. You start to slow down as the drum and your breath become one. Then you begin beating the drum twice on both the in and out breaths.

With each beat, your breath and heart rate slows down, and blood pressure decreases too. You feel yourself moving out of the stress mode you were in. You begin feeling lighter, and breathing deeper. The natural medication of drumming has created the desired inner state.

As we begin making the same choices that the ancients did, choosing natural modalities for healing, we find ourselves feeling healthier more of the time, and more closely attuned in with our inner rhythms and inner needs. The future, thus, becomes our present.

PART III

Bringing Drumming Into Your Life

Chapter Ten

Practical Techniques and Rhythm Activities

The following techniques, used in my drumming programs, can be practiced alone or with friends and family. My overall goal is to provide a gentle introduction to the drum through a series of exercises designed to give readers an experience of their inner rhythms as well as to experience the magic of drumming.

Each of these techniques can be used for multiple purposes. Certain techniques can be used for the self such as building concentration, enhancing creative expression, inducing meditative states, stress and anger management, and building self-esteem.

Other techniques can be used in relationships, such as increasing listening skills and increasing family harmony. Some techniques can be used in a group or work environment, such as for team-building. Many of these techniques overlap in their applications, for example, listening skills and stress management can be useful in a group or working environment.

Some exercises are geared for drumming facilitators and music therapists, others are geared more to the individual. In certain cases, I refer to those in attendance as participants. In these cases, I am gearing the technique for drumming facilitators.

A word of caution—many of the techniques listed can create an Alpha state through entrainment, others may speed up your heart rate, therefore, it would be advisable to consult with your physician before attempting any of these exercises.

The Heartbeat Rhythm

Recognized by many music therapists and drumming facilitators as one of the most vital healing rhythms to play on a drum, the heartbeat rhythm rightly is our starting point. The purpose of this exercise is twofold: to begin the process of acquainting yourself with your own inner rhythms and to experience the feeling of relaxation that this rhythm can create. This rhythm is the simplest of all to master. Some people prefer using a mallet or stick when playing the heartbeat rhythm. This exercise can be used for building concentration and as a stress management exercise.

Instructions

With a hand drum in close proximity, either held between your knees or close enough for you to play, close your eyes so there are no distractions. Put your hand on your heart or your wrist in order to get a feel for your own heartbeat. If you have trouble finding your heartbeat, don't panic! Simply imagine the sound of your heartbeat as you think it might be.

Now transfer the heartbeat rhythm to your voice, vocalizing the sound. Once you are comfortable vocalizing this beat, transfer it to your hand drum, either with a mallet or your hands. Try to continue this steady beat for at least five minutes. The longer you can play the heartbeat, the more you will find your body relaxing.

The Relationship-Heartbeat Rhythm

This is a wonderful exercise for couples who would like to feel more in in tune with each other. This technique may allow those individuals who practice this technique to feel a greater sense of oneness during the exercise. This exercise is wonderful for building intimacy, developing listening skills, and building concentration.

Instructions

This exercise begins with both individuals closing their eyes, breathing slowly and evenly while holding their respective hand drums. With the goal of creating two heartbeat rhythms sounding as one, each person begins by playing a heartbeat rhythm on his or her own drum. Both partners need to listen to and have the goal of moving in sync with what the other is playing. What often occurs in this exercise is that at one point you may no longer hear the other person's heartbeat rhythm. This occurs because you have both become entrained and are both beating the drum as one. You may want to initially set a time for how long to continue this exercise, though many people simply trust that when it is time to end, they will stop.

Improvisational Heartbeat Rhythm

In this technique one person plays a steady heartbeat rhythm while the other is given the freedom to explore his or her creativity through free-style improvisation. This technique can be done with two or more drummers. This exercise is wonderful for developing listening skills, building concentration and developing creative expression.

Instructions

This exercise begins with someone deciding who will play the heartbeat rhythm and who will improvise. The person who will play the heartbeat rhythm begins playing a very steady rhythm. Once the rhythm is steady, the other person has the freedom to explore his or her creative expression through improvising in and around the other's heartbeat rhythm.

It is very important that the person who is playing the heartbeat rhythm concentrate on that rhythm only and not get swayed by the other person who is improvising. It is equally important that the person improvising listen to the tempo of the heartbeat rhythm and try to stay within that beat. It is a very good idea to switch roles so that both individuals can experience both roles.

Heart Beat/Breath Syncopation

Through juxtaposing the rhythm of the heartbeat with the rhythm of the breath, individuals can begin creating more complex beats. This exercise can be done with one or more individuals. This exercise is wonderful for developing listening skills and creative expression.

Instructions

This exercise begins by a person creating the heartbeat rhythm as described above. Do the heartbeat rhythm for five minutes and then stop. Now become aware of the rhythm of your breath. Notice the difference between the rhythm of your breath and the heartbeat. Vocalize the rhythm of your breath and then transfer this to your drum. Do this for five minutes and then stop. Next, imagine how these two rhythms would sound if they were played together and vocalize this rhythm. Trust the sound you are creating and then transfer this sound to your drum. Accept whatever rhythm emerges and enjoy it.

The African Village

The African Village serves as a metaphor of creating non-verbal communication through feeling, hearing and listening to another. This is a group exercise, and it allows for spontaneous improvisation and creative self-expression. This exercise can be done with four or more individuals, though the more people who participate, the better. This exercise can be used for developing listening skills, building intimacy, increasing creative expression and team-building.

Instructions

Lower the lights and ask all individuals present to close their eyes. Tell everyone that they will all be travelling on a fantasy together into the jungles of Africa.

As Babatunde Olatunji tells us, in African villages the drum is used for the purpose of communication. In this exercise all participants are asked to imagine that they are each in their own African village. The two goals of this exercise are for the participants to communicate a series of feelings or thoughts through their drums to others and secondarily to develop a group conversation through participants both speaking and listening through their drums.

After giving your instructions, allow silence to descend upon the room. What generally occurs next is that someone will break the silence by playing his or her drum "message," and another participant will then respond to it. The drum voices often sound initially like raindrops throughout the room as one person calls and another responds. I find it helpful to give very little instructions as to how the "messages" should sound, allowing for complete and total spontaneity.

The drumming voices often escalate to a driving rhythm where everyone calls and responds simultaneously, creating an African "conference call." It is especially intriguing to include a variety of percussion instruments among the drums to allow for diverse flavors to be heard in the darkness. As the conference call continues, the African Village settles into a dominant rhythm. If there is no dominant rhythm, it may be important for the leader or facilitator to create a base or foundation through a steady beat or a heartbeat rhythm.

When the "call" is complete, one by one the drummers drop out and silence reigns again. Then have everyone listen to the quiet stillness and the inner rhythms of the breath and heartbeat as they return home from their timeless journey into Africa.

The Scat Orchestra

Scat is the use of nonsensical words to create rhythms and is a wonderful warm-up exercise to get participants familiar with rhythm. This exercise always provides a humorous environment for the joyful inner child to emerge. The goal of this exercise is help acquaint individuals with their inherent rhythmical abilities and to help individuals to get in touch with their creative mind. This exercise can be used for enhancing listening skills and team-building.

Instructions

Begin this exercise by doing a call and respond with scat phrases created spontaneously. A scat phrase can be any rhythmical statement that is made up of nonsense words. An example might be "skee bop ba doo bop." The facilitator would say this scat phrase and then point to the participants to imitate him or her. After a few of these very silly phrases and the laughter that always accompanies them, he or she hands out "scat cards." A scat card can be any card that has a particular scat phrase written on it. Though each scat card has its own words, the rhythms of all scat cards are similar so than an overall rhythm will permeate the room. Going around the room, have each person repeat his or her scat phrase in a looping fashion. Work your way around the room, assisting participants as they attempt to vocalize the nonsense words in front of them. The room begins to fill with a dominant vocalized scat rhythm that becomes more and more clear. Next, have everyone transfer the scat rhythms they are vocalizing into their drums as the room reverberates with the magic of improvisational drumming.

Drum Set Vocalizations

Like scat, this exercise uses vocalization in order to help non-drummers become more comfortable with their rhythmic sensibility. It also engages the joyful inner child as participants are invited to have fun and pretend they are playing a drum set. This exercise can be used to promote team building, inspire laughter and enhance listening skills.

Instructions

Begin by letting the participants know that they are going to learn to play a drum set. Next, inviting them to play this make-believe set of drums with you, demonstrate with a make-believe stick the motions and sounds of each part of the drum set.

Each drum in a drum set has a particular sound. Hit the snare drum while making a snare drum sound, then a tom-tom sound, bass drum, crash cymbal sound, ride cymbal sound and finally a hi-hat sound. With each part of the drum, I teach participants a movement and sound associated with that part of the drum. For instance, the hi-hat makes a hissing sound. The tom-tom creates a medium to low tone. The bass drum creates the lowest tone. The snare drum makes a more midrange sound. Once participants are introduced to their drum sets, do a call and respond where you create drumming phrases using all of the parts of the drum set, with corresponding physical motions. This creates lots of laughter, yet everyone can easily do it.

Next divide the room into sections, with each one creating a drum phrase that, when played together creates a syncopated drum set. The entire room becomes one drum set playing itself.

Clapping

This is a call and response exercise, the goal of which is to create a feeling of group unity. This exercise is similar to the Drum Set Exercise except it involves giving out syncopated clapping rhythms. This exercise can be used for developing listening skills and for team-building.

Instructions

Begin by introducing one of the most basic rhythm instruments known to human beings, the hands. Next begin with a call and response where the facilitator creates various rhythms which everyone follows. Next, divide the group into smaller sections, each having its own unique clapping rhythm, which meshes together with the others. Have them close their eyes and bathe in the rhythms they have created. Lastly, have them make up their own clapping rhythms.

Entrainment Exercise

The purpose of this exercise is to entrain the body and mind to a particular rhythm. This exercise is useful for stress management and creating meditative states.

Instructions

Begin by taking slow deep breaths. On every out-breath, hit the drum once as you match your breath to the beat of the drum. As you do this, you will find that your body relaxes in response to the rhythm of the drum.

Entrainment Exercise II

The purpose of this exercise to entrain your body and mind while someone else drums. This exercise is useful for stress management and for creating meditative states.

Instructions

In this exercise, ideal for couples, begin by deciding who will do the drumming and who will do the relaxing. The person who will be entrained should either lie down or find a comfortable position sitting up, close his or her eyes and begin taking slow, deep breaths. The drummer needs to watch the breath of the person who is being entrained. On every out-breath, the drummer will hit the drum. The goal is to have the person who is being entrained experience the drum and breath as one. An alternate way of doing this exercise is to have the drummer hit the drum on both the in-breath and the out-breath of the person who is being entrained to the drum. This begins to create the effect of breathing the drum and the drum breathing you.

Entrainment Exercise III

The purpose of this exercise is to use entrainment to energize or relax yourself. This exercise is useful for stress management and for creating meditative states.

Instructions

If you find that you are tired, hit a drum at a tempo that reflects the desired increased energy level, for instance, with a quick and steady beat. As your body entrains to the faster rhythm, undoubtedly you will start to feel more energized.

Conversely, if you want to relax, do the opposite. Play a slow and steady beat and watch your body relax and entrain to this slower rhythm.

Affirmations

When the hypnotic power of the drum is combined with powerful positive statements, or affirmations, the effects can be deep and long-lasting. Through focusing on a rhythm that echoes an affirmative statement, the subconscious is often able to internalize the positive statement, allowing an individual to more quickly access the change of thought or behavior desired.

In using the drum with affirmations, each syllable of the statement becomes a beat, each phrase becomes a rhythm. Hitting one drumbeat per syllable reinforces the affirmation and helps to imprint it in one's consciousness. This exercise is useful for building self-esteem, improving self-concept and creating positive beliefs.

Following are some suggestions for affirmations.

Affirmation Suggestions

I forgive myself and release my past.
I embrace the new.
I am good enough.
I am powerful, wise and strong.
I love myself, exactly as I am.
Joy flows into my life right now.
I am worthy and deserving.
I accept myself exactly as I am.
I love to love myself.
Peace is within.
I feel peace.
I deserve love.
I am a great success.
I forgive myself.

I release the past and embrace the new.
I am a drummer—powerful and strong.
Everything I do, makes me feel brand new.

Instructions

Repeat each phrase verbally a few times until you hear its particular rhythm. Then as you say the phrase out loud, play its rhythm on your drum. An easy way to determine the rhythm of the phrase is to play each syllable as a beat.

The most powerful affirmations will probably be the ones you make up for yourself. In creating an affirmation, think about a behavior or belief that you would like to change. Then, create a one sentence statement that reflects the new behavior or belief that you would like to incorporate into your life. Next, say this phrase over and over until the rhythm becomes apparent and repeat your affirmation aloud while drumming the syllables.

Releasing Emotions Into the Drum

The drum is the perfect vehicle for releasing negative emotions. I use the following exercise as a way to help individuals and groups release and transform their emotions. This exercise is useful for stress and anger management.

Instructions

Ask participants to practice drumming their emotions, including happiness, fear, sadness, and anger. Usually happiness is played as a series of rapid, syncopated beats. Fear might be expressed as staccato tappings. Sadness usually evokes slow, ponderous beats, while anger often becomes hard, loud, energetic drumming.

If a person is feeling a predominant emotion, the drum is a wonderful way to express that feeling.

If a participant is feeling sad, encourage them to play their sadness. This will help him or her to release the feeling. If the individual is angry, I recommend hitting the drum with a beater or stick so that the person doesn't injure him or herself. If the individual has a problem that persists, I would suggest consulting a music therapist or counselor to assist in the process.

Drumming Meditation

This exercise uses the drum to help an individual attain a meditative state. This exercise is useful for creating deep relaxation and developing meditative states.

Instructions

Find a comfortable position. Each time you take an in-breath say the number 1 inside of your mind while hit the drum once, on the out-breath, say the number 2 inside of your mind while hitting the drum once. No matter what thoughts impede your mind, continue to repeat the number 1 on the in-breath and two on the out-breath. The brain begins to entrain to the sound of the drum, and a meditative state can be reached. Other words can be substituted, such as "relaxing" on the in-breath, "relaxed" on the out-breath or "breath in" on the in-breath, "breath out" on the outbreath. To attain the deeper levels of meditation you may need to either record the drum or have someone else drum for you. Using the drum in this way, the drum becomes an ally of inner peace and deep concentration.

Drumming to Feel Your Power

This is a wonderful exercise for creating the feeling of inner strength. This exercise can be used for building self-esteem, improving self-concept and team-building.

Instructions

Close your eyes while holding a drum. Take a deep breath in, and as you breathe out, imagine your body relaxing. Begin hitting the drum slowly, and as you do, visualize yourself being alone, yet feeling strong. As if you had the power of the drum within you, become the drum. Imagine that as you hit the drum slowly, you are letting yourself move into the power of the drum so that each resounding sound is a reflection of the strength that you have within, that you are. You are powerful as the drum is. You are whole and complete as the drum is. You are the drum.

Drumming Away Your Stress

You can do this with a mallet or your hands. For this exercise it might be safer to choose a drum that uses a mallet due to the intensity you may use to hit the drum. This exercise can be used for stress management and team-building.

Instructions

Find a comfortable position with a hand drum in front of you. Think about your stressor(s). As you do, begin hitting your drum, imagining your stress exiting from your hands into the stick or mallet and going into the drum where it is transmuted into sound vibration and dissipated. Continue hitting the drum until you feel the stress is totally released.

Family Drumming Exercise

Find a day at least once a week when the members of your family can drum together. Through drumming together a family can create a greater feeling of unity and harmony by doing something fun together, and conflicts could find resolution through this form of nonverbal communication. Following is an exercise modeled after a counseling technique called "active listening." This technique is wonderful for creating family harmony and developing community.

Instructions

One family member begins this exercise by playing his or her predominant emotion on the drum. The remaining family members take turns reflecting back or "mirroring" the drum beats. If necessary, the first drummer replays the beats until everyone can reflect them back accurately. This activity continues until each family member has expressed his or her predominant emotion on the drum and each family member has reflected it back to the best of his or her ability. This exercise gives family members the comforting feeling of being heard and gives everyone in the family a "voice."

In addition, many of the previous techniques and those found in the following section, "Drumming Techniques from Music Therapy," would be appropriate and fun for use in a family drum circle.

Chapter Eleven

Drumming Exercises from Music Therapy

The following techniques are contributed by music therapist Tony Scarpa. They show ways to use the drum to enhance communication, concentration, listening skills, intimacy, and an understanding of the self. It is recommended that these techniques be used in the accompaniment of a music therapist.

Techniques of Empathy

These are techniques that allow an individual to feel heard and supported.

Synchronizing	This technique creates a feeling of connectedness.
	Play the rhythms that the other person is playing at the same time in unison.
Incorporating	This technique builds self-esteem as a person's creation is validated and built upon.
	Take a rhythmic phrase that a person is repeating and make it the basis of a composition.
Pacing	This technique allows a person to feel heard, builds listening skills.
	Match the other person's energy level. Do not play

the exact rhythms he or she is playing, but match the intensity.

Reflecting	This technique shows that you have empathy for the person's feelings.
	Match the attitudes, moods, and feelings of the other person such as happy, sad, angry.
Exaggerating	This technique can inject humor and provide perspective.
	Exaggerate what is being played, amplifying what the other person is doing.
Imitating	This technique creates a feeling of being heard and supported.
	Echo back what the person plays on the drum. Whatever his or her response is, play it back.

Techniques for Structuring

These are techniques that give form, shape or structure to what a person is playing on the drum.

Rhythmic Grounding	This technique builds self-esteem by changing chaos to a musical composition.
	Keep a basic beat for the person so that he or she can improvise on top of the beat.
Shaping	This technique helps to establish boundaries.
	Help the person find a beginning and end to the phrase they are improvising.

Techniques of Intimacy

These are techniques that build trust.

Sharing   This technique creates intimacy.

Both people play the same instrument while making eye contact.

Bonding   This technique deepens rapport and increases camaraderie.

Develop a rhythmic composition together which you play every time you drum. It becomes a theme or signature piece.

Elicitation Techniques

These techniques help to encourage participation and duration of playing.

Repeating   This technique helps to create a feeling of security and through repetition increases ones confidence that one has the ability to play the drum. Self-esteem is also increased.

Play the same rhythm or pattern over and over again.

Modeling   This technique builds confidence and self-esteem.

Demonstrate a rhythm and have another person repeat it.

Making Spaces This technique helps to build creativity and improvisational skills.

Leave spaces within the rhythmic structure for the other person to interject his or her rhythms.

Interjecting	This technique helps a person feel supported and metaphorically creates intimacy through building bridges.
	Fill in the spaces when the other person stops playing.
Extending	This technique aids in creating sense of completion.
	Add a rhythm to the end of someone's piece in order to create a sense of completion or structure.

Redirection Techniques

These techniques introduce change in an improvisation by redirecting tempo or introducing a different beat.

Differentiation	This technique increases concentration.
	Play a different rhythm from the one the other person is playing.
Modulation	This technique increases listening skills.
	Change the speed or intensity of the improvisation.
Intervene	This technique sets limits and creates boundaries.
	Interrupt or stop the other person's drumming if he or she is losing control.
Reacting	After drumming, talk about what the other person liked or didn't like and their reaction to the drumming.

The following questionnaire was devised by Jim Anderson as a way to help individuals gain information as to how rhythm impacts their life. Please feel free to fill this out and discover the influence rhythm has on your life.

WHAT ARE YOUR LIFE RHYTHMS?

What rhythms are you aware of in your life?

_____

_____

_____

Do you see yourself as being slow, medium, or fast in your thinking process? Also rank your feeling and behavior processes, in terms of slow, medium, or fast rhythm.

_____

_____

_____

Now rank each member in your family (thought, feeling, and behavior). Again use slow, medium, and fast, to describe their life rhythms.

_____

_____

_____

Describe your life tempo. What is a normal day like for you? Do you see yourself being in synchrony with the world, or do you usually feel more out-of-sorts with your environment?

_____

_____

_____

How does your life rhythm and tempo affect you? Others? How does it fit into the context of your family's tempo?

_____

_____

_____

Do you feel synchronized with your family in terms of thoughts, feelings and behaviors?

_____

_____

_____

Do you feel that your day-to-day rhythm is cohesive with who you are as a person? To what extent is your personal rhythm influenced by others?

_____

_____

_____

How is your life rhythm affected by situations and circumstances around you? How are you affected by people with extreme tempos, such as super slow or really fast?

_____
_____
_____

If you could play your life rhythm on a drum, how would it sound? Would it be loud or soft, busy or sparse? Would your song have many notes or few? What tempo would it be?

_____
_____
_____

Do you see your family as a cohesive synchronized unit? In what way? Are family members operating at different rhythms? Whose rhythms are dominant? Which member of the family does the family match pace with?

_____
_____
_____

Family rhythms, like life rhythms, are always changing. Family rhythms have dynamic patterns which are always in a constant state of flux. As family members, we all adjust life rhythms in order to get along together. In what ways do you find yourself adjusting your tempo to your family? Do you see these adjustments as healthy? In what ways do you see your family adjusting to your tempo of life?

_____
_____
_____

How do you see your family dynamics affecting your overall life rhythm? Are you staying true to yourself and making active choices of when to adjust your rhythm, or do you feel like you are constantly out of synchrony with yourself and everyone else?

_____

_____

_____

Have you ever felt bombarded by a million different things at the same time? Feeling rhythmically bombarded can create intense stress. In music and in life, polyrhythms (multiple rhythms occurring simultaneously) can create a sense of chaos. However, polyrhythms can also create a sense of flow and pleasure depending on how they are subjectively perceived. When a group of people are all trying to talk over the top of each other, a "stress polyrhythm" occurs. When a family is synchronized together in a conversation that allows room for each individual's rhythms to be expressed, a "flow polyrhythm" will occur. By developing an understanding of each other's rhythms and the way in which they interact, family members are better able to see how they affect, and are affected by others.

_____

_____

_____

How would you describe the rhythmic give and take process in your family?

_____

_____

_____

When someone around you is highly elevated, do you become excited? How about when your children are depressed? Do you see yourself as being enmeshed with their rhythms, or are you able to differentiate your rhythm in order to keep a sense of balance in your life?

_____
_____
_____

Matching life rhythms is a natural process defined by biological sciences as "entrainment." By entraining with one another we validate each other's experiences. Often when people are experiencing a conflict they will automatically escalate anger rhythms together, or rhythmically disengage and become dissociated from each other. This process of de-synchronization usually occurs emotionally at an unconscious level. Are you aware of any ongoing issues that create a lack of synchrony in your family? In your life?

_____
_____
_____

Chapter Twelve

Conclusion

It is my belief that, as a society, we need to move towards using more of the tools of our natural environment to become more at home with our planet, and the use of rhythm to facilitate this is but one part in this great orchestration.

You have read about the latest information on the power of rhythm to affect health from medical doctors, researchers, psychologists, psychiatrists and therapists. You have read stories of individuals who have had miraculous experiences through rhythm, either through playing a drum, a rhythm instrument, a melodic instrument played rhythmically, or listening to a metronome or even a tape of rhythm. You have read about the power of the drum to help individuals with both psychological and physiological maladies. It is my hope that you may now be thinking of how you, your family, and your friends can use this healing vehicle.

It is my further hope that as you explore the many ways that the drum can touch you, you will go out into the world to find your own drum, the one that calls to you, and use it to benefit you in whatever way you choose, or that you find a music therapist to work with you in exploring your deeper emotions or a drumming facilitator to usher in the experience of rhythm into your life.

I have provided a reference list so that you may contact the many individuals, including researchers, music therapists and drumming facilitators, who contributed to this book, as well as organizations, and various products that can assist you in this path. I would love to hear from you through my website or e-mail address (as listed in the resource section) if you have any stories or thoughts regarding how the drum has had a positive impact on your life.

Of course, there may still be a part of you that, despite the research, remains skeptical, and I especially invite that aspect to experience the drum, for reading this book will provide you with only an intellectual exercise of rhythm. It is only through actually playing a drum or listening to rhythm that you will be able to experience what this burgeoning field is all about. Without the experience of actually taking part in this phenomenon, you will not provide yourself with the true possibility of experiencing its effects on your being.

As you read this book, you may have noticed inspirations or impulses that you may have either followed or censored—impulses to find a drumming group, buy a drum or call a music therapist, for example. Of course, only you know what is right for you, but this writer encourages you nevertheless to follow your impulses, for it is when we follow our impulses that we get to experience our spirit in action. The skeptic has a voice that is meant to discern truth from fiction, and the skeptic's voice will remain loud until it is provided with an experience that shows it the opposite.

Indeed, in the area of rhythm and health, much more research is needed, for without research our skeptical minds remain at large. Research provides the grounding and evidence we need to validate our own inner experience and knowing. Our subjective ideas provide us with an inner knowing, but unless that inner knowing is validated by research, there is room for doubt.

Nevertheless, you have made the choice to read this book and explore the thoughts and feelings it engenders. It is my hope now that you take the next step—finding a drum, making your sound, and discovering the power of the drum to heal yourself psychologically, physiologically or spiritually. In some ways, though you have completed this book, your journey may just have begun. On the other hand, if you just use the drum and rhythm to add some fun to your life, I will feel that my efforts have been more than worthwhile.

Some of you may have preferred a book that included research in a less casual form, yet it was my desire to write a book that both the layman and the researcher could understand. It was my hope that this book reflect the very basic nature of rhythm itself, to be simple and fun, yet expansive and transforming.

For what can be experienced through the drum is the power of rhythm that exists within us. The drum and its rhythms unlock some of the most positive qualities we have as human beings—the need to connect with others, the expression of our creative selves, the exhilaration of joy and play and the capacity to heal. The natural drum is an accessible tool available to all of us. May you become the drummer that you already are.

REFERENCES

Aigen, Kenneth. "The Voice of the Forest: A Conception of Music for Music Therapy," *Music Therapy* 10(1)(1991):77-98.

Aigen, Kenneth. *Paths of Development in Nordoff-Robbins Music Therapy*. Gilsum, NH: Barcelona Publishers, 1998.

Aigen, Kenneth (in press). "Popular Musical Styles in Nordoff-Robbins Clinical Improvisation," *Music Therapy Perspectives*. [Will be published in Spring 2001).

Aldridge, David. *Music Therapy Research and Practice in Medicine: From Out of the Silence*. London: Jessica Kingsley Publishers, 1996.

Ansdell, Gary. *Music for Life: Aspects Of Creative Music Therapy with Adult Clients*. London: Jessica Kingsley Publishers, 1995.

Assiogoli, Roberto. *Psychosynthesis*. USA: Hobbs Dorman & Company, 1965.

Bernstein, Barry, and Gary Johnson. "Rhythm Playing Characteristics in Persons with Severe Dementia Including Those with Probable Alzheimer's Type," *Journal of Music Therapy* (1995): 113-131.

Bower, Bruce. "The Character of Cancer," *Science News*, 131; 1987, 120-121.

Burke, M.A. "Effects of Physioacoustic Intervention on Pain Management of Postoperative Gynecological Patients," *Music Vibration* (1997): 107-123.

Burt, John. "Distant Thunder: Drumming with Vietnam Veterans," *Music Therapy Perspectives 13* (1995): 110-112.

Burt, John, and Christine Stevens. "Drum Circles: Theory and Application in the Mental Health Continuum," *Continuum 2* (Summer 1997): 171-184.

Butler, C.F. and P.J. Butler. "Physioacoustic Therapy with Cardiac Surgery Patients," *Music Vibration* (1997): 197-207.

Butler, C. F. "Physioacoustic Therapy with Post Surgical and Critically Ill Patients," In C. Dileo (Ed.) *Music Therapy and Medicine: Theoretical and Clinical Applications*. The American Music Therapy Association, Inc., Silver Spring, MD. (1999): 31-40.

Butler, C. F. "Physioacoustics: The Sound Treatment of Pain and

Stress," Institute on Pain and Stress Management. *First National Association of Music Therapists Convention,* Case Weston Reserve University, Cleveland, Ohio. 1998.

Clair, Alicia Ann, Barry Bernstein, and Gary Johnson. "Rhythm Playing Characteristics In Persons With Severe Dementia Including Those With Probable Alzheimer's Type," *Journal of Music Therapy,* (1995): 113-131.

Lee, Colin. *Music at the Edge: The Music Therapy Experience of a Musician with AIDS.* London: Routledge, 1996.

Lehikoinen, P. *The Physioacoustic Method.* Kalamazoo, Michigan: Next Wave, Inc. (unpublished), 1990.

Lehikoinen, P., H. Naukkarinen, T. Paakkari, and N. Saukkonnen. "The Physioacoustic Method In the Treatment of Psychic Anxiety," *Fifth International Congress of Psychophysiology,* Budapest, Hungary, 1990.

Llinas, R. and U. Ribary. "Coherent 40-Hz Oscillation Characterized Dreamlike States in Humans," *Neurobiology,* 90 (1993): 2078-2081.

Longhofer, Jeffrey Ph.D. and Jerry Floersch, LMSW. "African Drumming and Psychiatric Rehabilitation," *Psychosocial Rehabilitation Journal* 16.4 (1993): 3-9.

Marano, Hara Estroff. "The Power of Play," *Psychology Today,* July-August 1999: 37-40, 68-69.

Mauer, Sr., Ronald L., V.K. Kumar, Lisa Woodside, Lisa Pekala, J. Ronald. "Phenomenological Experience In Response To Monotonous Drumming And Hypnotizability," *American Journal of Clinical Hypnosis* (1997): 130-141.

Neher, A., Ph.D. "A Physiological Explanation Of Unusual Behavior In Ceremonies Involving Drums," *Human Biology* 34 (1962): 151-160.

Nissenen, A. and P. Kivinen. *University of Kuopio Hypertension Study.* (From the Finnish Literature) (1990).

Nordoff, Paul and Clive Robbins. *Creative Music Therapy.* New York: John Day & Co., 1977.

Nordoff, Paul and Clive Robbins. *Therapy In Music For Handicapped Children.* London: Gollancz., 1971; 1973; 1992.

Pavlicevic, Mercedes. *Music Therapy in Context: Music, Meaning and Relationship.* London & Philadelphia: Jessica Kingsley

Publishers, 1997.

Rechtschaffen, Stephan, M.D. *Time Shifting*. New York: Doubleday Publishing Group, 1996.

Redmond, Layne. *When the Drummers Were Women: The Spiritual History of Rhythm*. New York: Crown Publishing, 1997.

Roskam, Kay Sherwood, Ph.D., RMT-BC. *Feeling the Sound: The Influence of Music on Behavior*. San Francisco: San Francisco Press, 1993.

Roskam, Kay Sherwood, Ph.D., RMT-BC. "Music Making As Therapy At Harbor View Adolescent Center," *Think Drums*, Hollywood, CA: Remo, Inc. (1995).

Ruud, E. *Music Therapy: Improvisation, Communication, and Culture*. Gilsum, N.H.: Barcelona Publishers, 1998.

Seashore, Carl E. *Psychology of Music*. New York: McGraw Hill Publishers, 1938.

Stevens, Christine K., and John W. Burt. "Drum Circles: Theory and Application in the Mental Health Treatment Continuum," *The Journal for the Association of Ambulatory Health Care* (1997) 4.2.

Thaut, M. "The Use Of Auditory Rhythm and Rhythmic Speech To Aid Temporal Muscular Control In Children With Gross Motor Dysfunction," *Journal of Music Therapy* 22.3 (1985): 108-128.

Thaut, M., S. Schleiffers and W. Davis. "Analysis of EMG Activity In Biceps and Triceps Muscle In An Upper Extremity Gross Motor Task Under the Influence of Auditory Rhythm," *Journal of Music Therapy* 28.2 (1991): 64-88.

Wagenheim, Jeff. (Mickey Hart quoted in "The Rhythm Method," *New Age Magazine* January/February 1999: 76.

Wagenheim, Jeff. "The Rhythm Method," *New Age Magazine* January/February 1999: 76-80.

Wigram, T. "The Effect of VA Therapy on Multiply Handicapped Adults With High Muscle Tone and Spasticity," *Music Vibration* (1997): 57-68.

Wigram, T. "The Effect of Vibroacoustic Therapy Compared With Music and Movement Based Physiotherapy on Multiply Handicapped Patients with High Muscle Tone and Spasticity," *Music Vibration* (1997): 69-85.

RHYTHM AND PERCUSSION RESOURCES

Books

Byrne, Patrick F. *Instant Drumming for the Table Top Drummer.*
Wisconsin: Hal Leonard Publishing Corporation, 1993.

Chernoff, John Miller. *African Rhythms & African Sensibility:
Aesthetics & Social Action in African Musical Idioms.*
University of Chicago Press, 1979.

Crowe, Barbara, and Barry Bernstein,. *Cost Effective Activity
Programs for Older Adults with Dementia.* (Booklet, Book,
Video-Marketing Kit.)
American Music Therapy Association, 1995.

Clynes, Manfred and Janis Walker. *Music, Mind and Brain.*
(Chapter on "Neurologic Functions of Rhythm, Time and
Pulse in Music, pp. 171-216). New York: Plenium Press,
1983.

Diallo, Yaya, and Mitchell Hall. *The Healing Drum: African
Wisdom Teachings.* Vermont: Destiny Books, 1989.

Dworsky, Allen and Betsy Sansby. *Conga Drumming: A Beginner's
Guide to Playing with Time.* MN: Dancing Hands Music, 1994.

Evans, James R., and Manfred Clynes. *Rhythm in Psychological,
Linguistic and Musical Process.* NA: Charles C. Thomas Publishers, 1986.

Gerard, Charley and Marty Sheller. *Salsa!: The Rhythm of Latin
Music.* Reno, NV: White Cliffs Media, 1989.

Hart, Mickey, Jay Stevens and Fredric Lieberman. *Drumming at
the Edge of Magic.* New York: Harper Collins, 1990.

Hart, Mickey and Fredric Lieberman. *Planet Drum: A Celebration
of Percussion and Rhythm.* New York: Harper Collins, 1991.

Hawkins, Holly. *The Heart of the Circle–A Guide to Drumming.*
California: The Crossing Press, 1999

Hull, Arthur. *Drum Circle Spirit: Facilitating Human Potential
Through Rhythm.* Reno, NV: White Cliffs Media, 1998.

Klower, Tom. *The Joy of Drumming.* ND: Binkey Kok.

Locke, David. *Drum Gahu: An Introduction to African Rhythm.*
Reno, NV: White Cliffs Media, 1998.

Luth, Gay Gaer. *Biological Rhythms in Human and Animal Physiol-*

ogy. New York: Dover Publications Inc., 1971.

Mason, Bernard S. *How to Make Drums, Tom-Toms and Rattles, Primitive Percussion Instruments for Modern Use.* New York: Dover Publications, Inc., 1974.

McNeil, William H. *Keeping Together in Time: Dance and Drill in Human History.* Massachusetts: Harvard University Press, 1995.

Olatunji, Babatunde. *The Beat of My Drum*. Temple Universty Press, (Release Date: Fall, 2000).

Redmond, Layne. *When the Drummers Were Women*. New York: Crown Publishing, 1997.

Reuer, Barbara, Barbara Crowe, and Barry Bernstein. *Rhythm For Life: Best Practice in Music Therapy: Utilizing Group Percussion Strategies for Promoting Volunteerism in the Well Older Adult.* American Music Therapy Association, 1995

Wilson, Sule Greg. *The Drummer's Path: Moving the Spirit with Ritual and Traditional Drumming.* Vermont: Destiny Books, 1992

CDs/Audiotapes

Assorted Artists. *The Big Bang* (RACS 3402).

Barry Bernstein. *Spirals—Unwinding for Vitality and Health* (RCD 3206).

Randy Crafton. *Inner Rhythms* (RCD 3185).

Mickey Hart. *At the Edge* (RCD 10124/RACS).

Mickey Hart and Taro Hart. *Music to be Born By* (RCD 20112/ RACS).

Mickey Hart, Airto Moreira, and Flora Purim. *Dafos* (RCD 10108/RACS).

Baba Olatunji. Drums of Passion: *The Invocation* (RCD 10102/ RACS).

Baba Olatunji. *Drums of Passion: The Beat.* (RCD 10107/RACS).

Layne Redmond. *Roots of Awakening* (RCD 931).

Layne Redmond. *Being in Rhythm*; Interworld (RCD 927).

Layne Redmond and the Mob of Angels. *Since the Beginning* (RCD 809042/CS 904).

Videotapes

John Bergamo. *The Art and Joy of Hand Drumming.* (vjb01).
John Bergamo and Friends. *Finding Your Way with Hand Drums* (vjb02).
Brad Dutz. *Have Fun Playing Hand Drums* (vho257)
Jim Greiner. *Community Drumming for Health and Happiness* (lpv115n)
Arthur Hull. *Guide to Endrummingment* (vah01)
Babatunde Olatunji. *African Drumming* (vbo01)
Layne Redmond. *A Sense of Time* (vho146).
Layne Redmond. Ritual Drumming (vlr01)
Layne Redmond with Tommy Brunjes. *Rhythmic Wisdom* (vh312).
Jerry Steinholtz. *The Essence of Playing Congas* (vjs01).
Glen Velez. The Fantastic World of Frame Drums. (vgv01).

Percussion Products

Boomwhackers
   www.boomwhackers.com
   Tuned percussion tubes
Jamtown
   www.jamtown.com
   Rhythm products
Latin Percussion (LP Music)
   www.lpmusic.com
   Percussion products, videos and other items
Remo, Inc.
   www.remousa.com
   Percussion products, videos and other items.
West Music
   www.westmusic.com
   Music therapy materials.

Researchers

Dr. Burt, John, MCAT, MT-BC
   e-mail: johnburt@prodigy.net
   phone: 970-482-4334
Barry Bernstein, MT-BC
   e-mail: nada@unicom.net
   website: www.healthysounds.com
   phone: 913-888-5517
   fax: 913-888-8204
Martha Burke, MS, MT- BC,
   The Center for Music Therapy Research, Greenville, N.C.
   e-mail: mburke@geeksnet.com
Charles F. Butler M.D. Ph.D.,
   Michigan State University,
   Kalamazoo Campus, Kalamazoo MI
   e-mail: CButler1@prodigy.net
Deforia Lane, Ph.D.
   Director Ireland Cancer Center
   Case Western Reserve University, Cleveland OH
   e-mail: deforialane@usa.net
David Sanders
   Physioacoustic Project Engineer,
   Minneapolis MN
   e-mail: dodave@earthlink.net
Dr. Petri Lehikoinen
   Sibelius Academy
   Helsinki, Finland
   e-mail: plehikoi@siba.fi
Riina Raudsik, M.D., Director
   Juri Medical Center,
   Juri, Estonia
   e-mail: jyritkoy@online.ee
Christine Stevens, MSW, MT-BC
   e-mail: cstevens@remo.com
   website: www.ubdrumcircles.com
   phone: 970-416-8974
Dr. Michael Thaut

Director, Center for Biomedical Research in Music
Colorado State University
Fort Collins, CO 80523
Dr. Connie Tomaino
    Director, Music Therapy
    Institute for Music and Neurologic Function
    Beth Abraham Health Services
    612 Allerton Avenue
    Bronx, New York 10467
    e-mail: ctomaino@bethabe.org
Tony Wigram, Ph.D.,
    Director of Doctoral Studies,
    University of Aalborg, Denmark
    e-mail: tony@musik.auc.dk

Drumming Facilitators

Jim Anderson, MS, MFT
    e-mail: JimDrumz@aol.com
    website: www.DrumsAndPercussion.com
    phone: 909-549-9400
    fax: 909-549-0549
Barry Bernstein, MT-BC
    e-mail: nada@unicom.net
    website: www.drumming-about-you.com
    phone: 913-888-5517
    fax: 913-888-8204
Bob Bloom
    e-mail: bb@drumming-about-you.com
    website: www.drumming-about-you.com
    phone: 860-429-9280
Nathan Brenowitz, MS
    e-mail: life@ulster.net
    website: www.maximal.nu/brenpp
    phone: 914-679-6855
Randy Crafton
    e-mail: crafton@earthdrum.com
    website: www.craftone.com

phone: 201-653-0986
Robert Lawrence Friedman, MA
  e-mail: rlf@stress-solutions.com
  website: www.stress-solutions.com
    www.drumming-event.com
  phone: 212-229-7779
  fax: 718-793-6326
Rob Gottfried
  e-mail: ROBTD@connix.com
  website: rob-the-drummer.com
  phone: 860-232-4044
  fax: 860-231-7470
Jim Greiner
  e-mail: jgreiner@cruzio.com
  website: www.handsondrum.com
  phone 831-462-3786
Arthur Hull
  e-mail: drum@drumcircle.com
  website: www.drumcircle.com
  phone: 831-458-1946
Flossie Ierardi, MM, MT-BC
  e-mail: fmi@bellatlantic.net
  phone: 215-637-2077
Heather MacTavish
  e-mail: rhythms@dnai.com
  website: www.newrhythms.org
  phone: 415-435-4870
  fax: 415-435-4878 / 505-442-3786
Baba Olatunji
  website: www.babaolatunji.com
  phone: 212-724-2118
Happy Shel
  website: www.drums.org
  phone: 214-823-DRUM (3786)
  alt. 214-824-2038
Christine Stevens, MT-BC
  website: www.ubdrumcircles.com
  phone: 970-416-8974

Drumming Programs

Jim Anderson, MS, MFT
   Rhythm-Power!
   e-mail: JimDrumz@aol.com
   website: www.DrumsAndPercussion.com
   phone: 909-549-9400
   fax: 909-549-0549
   Rhythm-Power! runs corporate and youth drum therapy
   seminars.
Barry Bernstein, MT-BC
   Healthy Sounds
   e-mail: nada@unicom.net
   website: www.healthysounds.com
   phone: 913-888-5517
   fax: 913-888-8204
   Healthy Sounds directed by noted music therapist Barry
   Bernstein, MT-BC, promotes wellness, team-building, creativity and communication through the use of hand drumming
   and other rhythm-based activities.
Bob Bloom
   Drumming About You
   e-mail: bb@drumming-about-you.com
   website: www.drumming-about-you.com
   phone: 860-429-9280
   Bob Bloom is the founder and director of "Drumming About
   You", a participatory drumming program that is accessible to
   all age groups, and is inclusive of people of challenge.
Steve Collins
   Loud Joy
   e-mail: scollins@loudjoy.com
   website: www.loudjoy.com
Robert Lawrence Friedman, MA
   Stress Solutions, Inc.
   Drumming Away Stress(r)
   Drumming Away Anger(tm)
   Drum Circles For Health(tm)
   e-mail: rlf@stress-solutions.com

website: www.stress-solutions.com
             www.drumming-event.com
phone: 212-229-7779
Robert Lawrence Friedman is the founder of Drumming Away
Stress, currently Stress Solutions, Inc. The purpose of his
organization is to use drumming events as vehicles for creating
meaning and purpose, enhancing communication, team-
building, creating celebration, expressing emotion and experiencing joy.
Tom Gill
  Rhythm For Unity
  website: www.execpc.com/~tgill/hodrum
  phone: 414-476-6986
Jim Greiner
  Hands-on! Drumming(r) Programs
  e-mail: jgreiner@cruzio.com
  website: www.handsondrum.com
  phone: 831-462-3786
  Jim Greiner is a nationally-known touring percussion and
  educator who leads team-building, drumming events and
  celebrations for corporations, conferences and communities
  through his company, Hands-On! Drumming(r) Events.
Arthur Hull
  Community Building in Community Festivals
  Spirit-Building in Colleges and Conferences
  Team-Building in Corporations
  Unity Through Diversity
  Village Music Circles Facilitators Playshop
  e-mail: drum@drumcircle.com
  website: www.drumcircle.com
  phone: 831-458 1946
  Arthur Hull, author of Drum Circle Spirit, is recognized as the
  father of the community drum circle movement.
Heather MacTavish
  New Rhythms Foundation
  phone: 415-435-4870
  website: www.newrhythms.org
  Heather MacTavish is a drumming facilitator who works with

elders and those with special needs and is the founder of New Rhythms Foundation.

Karin Meidel/Shirley Borchardt
  Pearlwizard Percussion
  website: www.pearlwizard.comShira Rae
  phone: 310-659-1093

Shira Rae
  DRUMMING FOR EVERYONE!
  e-mail   ShiraRae@aol.com
  phone: 856-728-5549

Rob Gottfried
  Rob-the Drummer Educational Programs Inc.
  e-mail: ROBTD@connix.com
  website(s):   rob-the-drummer.com
  phone: 860-232-4044
  fax: 860-231-7470

Rob's program themes are pro-arts, pro-sports, anti-substance abuse, self-esteem, performances worldwide with additional attention to goal-oriented thinking, self-reliance, need for practice, using a natural rather than artificial way to change the way you feel—for audiences from elementary through college and public family events.

Happy Shel
  Drums Not Guns
  website: www.drums.org
  phone: 214-823-DRUM (3786)
  alt.   214-824-2038

Christine Stevens, MT-BC
  Upbeat Drum Circles
  Music and the Mirror – "Diversity Training Through Sound and Self-Reflection"
  e-mail: cstevens@remo.com
  website: www.ubdrumcircles.com
  phone: 970-416-8974

Upbeat Drum Circles creatively uses drumming and music to enhance the collaborative and human elements of health and wellness, music therapy, conference events, diversity training, team-building, and women's empowerment.

Earth Drum Council
    Morwen Two-Feathers
    e-mail;   edc@earthdrum.com
    website: www.earthdrum.com
    phone: 978-371-2502
Unity with a Beat
    Barry Bernstein, MT-BC
    Randy Crafton
    e-mail: crafton@earthdrum
    web site: www.craftone.com
    The Unity With a Beat weekend retreat program has been
    utilized by companies, health care facilities and schools to
    enhance team effort in discovering more effective listening,
    conflict resolution and stress management skills.
John Walter (United Kingdom)
    DrumCrazy and Dragonfly Theatre
    e-mail: jwalter@drumcrazy.co.uk
    website: www.drumcrazy.co.uk

Music Therapists

Dr. Kenneth Aigen
    e-mail: kenneth.aigen@nyu.edu
Barry Bernstein, MT-BC
    e-mail: nada@unicom.net
    website(s):   www.healthysounds.com
    phone: 913-888-5517
    fax: 913-888-8204
Tom Dalton, MT-BC
    e-mail: tdalton@hpbc.com
Flossie Ierardi, MM, MT-BC
    e-mail: fmi@bellatlantic.net
    phone: 215-637-2077
Shira Rae, CMT
    e-mail   ShiraRae@aol.com or
    phone: 856-728-5549
Tony Scarpa, MA, CMT
    phone: 516-561-8273

Christine Stevens, MSW, MT-BC
    e-mail: christine@ubdrumcircles.com
    website(s):   www.ubdrumcircles.com
    phone: 970-310-8010
Alan Turrey, MT-BC
    e-mail: alan.turrey@nyu.edu
    phone: 212-998-5151
Additional music therapists in your area can be located through:
The American Music Therapy Association
    phone: 301-589-3300
    web site: www.namt.com

Clinicians

Dr. John Burt, Ph.D., MCAT, RMT-BC
    e-mail: johnburt@prodigy.net
    Phone: 970-482-4334
Barry L. Quinn, Ph.D.
    e-mail: mindspa@nail.net
    web site: www.nail.net/mindspa
    Phone: 719-635-3805
    Fax: 719-635-3805

Performer/Teacher

Randy Crafton
    e-mail: crafton@earthdrum.com
    website: www.craftone.com
Layne Redmond
    e-mail: layne@svic.net
    web site: www.layneredmond.com

Drumming Mailing Lists

www.djembe-l@egroups.com
www.drumcircles@listbot.com
www.drums.org
www.egroups.com/community/handdrumming

www.egroups.com/group/Learn_the_djembe
www.jembe-list@lyris.wesleyan.edu
www.egroups.com/community/Drum-Circle
www.egroups.com/community/RhythmHealing
www.egroups.com/community/djembe-l
Djembe Ireland
   "Dedicated to Bringing African Music and Culture to Ireland"
   www.gofree.indigo.ie/~djembe
   www.onelist.com/community/Djembe-Ireland
   www.egroups.com/community/RhythmHealing

Additional Web Sites

Conditions
   Alzheimer's Association
   www.alz.org
American Parkinson's Disease Association
   www.apdaparkinson.com/
The Autism Society of America
   www.autism-socity.org
National Association of Downs Syndrome
   www.nads.org/
National Down Syndrome Society
   www.ndss.org/
National Multiple Sclerosis Society
   www.nmss.org/
   National Parkinsons Foundation
   www.parkinson.org/
National Stroke Association
   www.stroke.org/
Williams Syndrome Association
   www.williams-syndrom.org

Organizations

All One Tribe Foundation
   A non-profit organization whose mission is to educate people

worldwide about the physical, psychological and spiritual
benefits of drumming.

American Music Therapy Association
A comprehensive site dedicated to advancing public awareness of music therapy
www.amta.org

Certified Board of Music Therapists
Evaluates individuals who wish to enter, continue and/or
advance in the discipline of music therapy
www.cbmt.com

Drums Not Guns
A non-profit, non-discriminatory membership organization
devoted to stopping violence through the power of percussion.
www.drums.org

MUSE in the Schools (Musicians United for Superior Education)
Provide rhythm and dance-based programs for grade schools.
www.musekids.org/schools.html

Music Education and Music Therapy for Children and Youth
with Disabilities Network
Resource site with information, activities, resources to aid in
music education and music therapy for students with disabilities.
www.busboy.sped.ukans.edu

Music for People
Dedicated to promoting music as a means of self-expression.
www.musicforpeople.org

Nordoff-Robbins Music Therapy
Provides detailed information regarding the Nordoff-Robbins
approach to music therapy.
www.nyu.edu/education/music/robbins

Percussive Arts Society (PAS)
Provides drummers, percussionists with information, research,
publications.
www.pas.org

Prelude Music Therapy
Resources for music therapy, information, services and
products. http://home.att.net/~bkbrunk/index.html

Institutions Mentioned in the Book

Center for Biomedical Research in Music
    Colorado State University
    Fort Collins, CO 80523
    www.colostate.edu/Depts/CRBM
Horizons Bereavement Center
    A Program of Hospice of Palm Beach County, Inc.
    5300 East Avenue
    West Palm Beach
    Florida 33407
    www.hpbc.com
Institute for Music and Neurologic Function
    Beth Abraham Health Services
    612 Allerton Avenue
    Bronx, New York 10467
    www.bethabe.org
National Center for Post-Traumatic Stress Syndrome
    VA Medical Center
    950 Campbell Avenue
    West Haven, CT 06516

INDEX

About the Author

Robert Lawrence Friedman, MA, Psychotherapist, Remo Artist, Drumming Facilitator, Certified Psychosynthesis Practitioner, is affiliated with St. Mary's Hospital Complementary Therapy Department located in New Jersey. Mr. Friedman is the President of Stress Solutions, Inc., a firm based on the East Coast which offers, among other health-related programs, drumming events for adults, young adults and children, including Drumming Away Stress(r), Drum Circles for Health(tm), The Drumming Celebration(tm) and Drumming Away Anger(tm). He has provided his programs to major corporations, hospitals, school, nursing homes, detention centers and conferences and has appeared on numerous radio and television programs.

Additional copies of *The Healing Power of the Drum* by Robert Lawrence Friedman, along with the complete title list of books about music from White Cliffs Media, may be purchased at book and music stores everywhere, by calling 1-800-359-3210 to order, or online at http://www.wc-media.com.